CANNING GOLD

Northern New England's Sweet Corn Industry

A HISTORICAL GEOGRAPHY

Paul B. Frederic

University Press of America,® Inc.
Lanham · New York · Oxford

Copyright © 2002 by
University Press of America,® Inc.
4720 Boston Way
Lanham, Maryland 20706
UPA Acquisitions Department (301) 459-3366

12 Hid's Copse Rd.
Cumnor Hill, Oxford OX2 9JJ

ISBN 0-7618-2199-6 (cloth: alk. paper)

To Corn Shop Workers (Canners of Gold)

Zella,
This is another
chance to live
part of your new
Sharon youth again;
Regards,
Paul
June 22, 2002

In polar seas, on the pyramid of Cheops and in the shadow of the Great Sphinx, in cabin and in forecastle on the deep, in cotton and rice fields of the South, in settlement and in city, on mountain and in canyon of the far West, on the table of the college president and in the hut of the African..., a luxurious edible alike to the Vassar graduate and Mexican... among all races and nationalities, everywhere is found and enjoyed preserved canned sweet corn which comes from the State of Maine.

Bangor (Maine) Industrial Journal 6 June 1888

McDonald's Restaurant...not a clue to suggest...the former site of one of Farmington's major industries, Franklin Farms Products Company, that went into business in 1921 and finally closed their doors in 1968 (the last Northern New England cannery to pack sweet corn).

Roy Darlington *Farmington (Maine) Franklin Journal* 10 March 1995

Contents

Figures

Tables

Acknowledgements

My early school years, through undergraduate degree, were spent in corn shop towns; Starks, New Sharon, and Farmington, Maine. I became familiar with the people and the workings of these communities. As my education as a geographer evolved, I kept thinking of how canning sweet corn linked small villages to the larger world. Mentors Myron Starbird, Albert Mitchell, Campbell Pennington, David Smith, Jean Gottmann, John Rooney, Sam Hillard, Curt Roseman, Fred Foster and John Jakle encouraged me to think about the big picture without losing track of all the local images. Although I have never taken a course from them, Carl Sauer, John Hudson, Mike Troughton, Howard Gregor, Bob LeBlanc, Bill Wallace, Tom Hubka, Wilber Zelinsky and John Fraser Hart, have given me much to consider when trying to understand how and why places change over time. Many people have encouraged and assisted me in this study. Marshall Edwards and Richard Gould provided technical insight about how to run corn shops. Betty Farnham Gould and Robert Wimble were outstanding help in suggesting research contacts in New Hampshire and Vermont. Twenty-seven Northern New England newspapers assisted by running a request for former corn shop workers to contact me. Berry Bishop, Tom Freese and David McLaughlin gave me great tours of their old corn factories. I interviewed seventy-five individuals who were a source of wonderful stories and helpful information. My Mother, Madge, and late Father, Glenn, as well as other family members encouraged me to pursue the canning gold story. I am grateful to John Wiley for permission to reprint substantial portions of *Sweet Corn* by Walter A Huelsen, New York: Interscience Publishers (1954). Permission to use materials from the files of B & M (Division of B & G, Foods), Maine Public Radio, Liberty Graphics, Marshall Edwards, Richard Gould, Ephraim Jillson, Madge Frederic, Gladys Lovell, David Sanderson, Peter Soule and Mary Croswell is appreciated and added much to this work. Many others, who are cited in the notes, gave authorization to use portions of their conservations with me.

A sabbatical leave from the University of Maine at Farmington allowed me time to work on this project. Richard P. Talbot aided me in organizing and understanding interview generated data. Fred Dearnley provided advice and assistance on photographic matters. Kathy Stevens helped transcribe interviews.

I thank Richard Condon, Frank Hodges, Matt Bampton, Jon Oplinger, John Jakle, John Fraser Hart and Jay Hoar, for reading and making helpful comments on early drafts of this book.

Special sainthood status is deserved for my wife, Liz, a geographer, who has been my cartographer, camera-ready typist, proof-reader, and field assistant. She was also the chief cheerleader when the game was difficult.

Despite excellent help and advice, any mistakes in this work are my responsibility.

Chapter 1

Introduction

I recall the discomforting silence while trying to come up with an acceptable icebreaker as the elder scholar across the desk watched me in a sort of relaxed curiosity. How should I, a first year geography master's student, a farm kid from Maine, take advantage of this opportunity to spend twenty minutes with the sage of cultural geography, Carl Sauer?[1] It was the spring of 1967 and Sauer was making his last pilgrimage through the Midwest, which included a series of lectures at Southern Illinois University in Carbondale, where, at that time, I was struggling to select a thesis topic. Sauer's disciple, Campbell Pennington, who was my academic advisor, had encouraged this meeting with the great mentor to discuss two ideas floating in my head. After what seemed an eternity, Dr. Sauer took mercy on my uncomfortable demeanor and asked, "What aspect of geography is of interest?" "Agriculture" was the reply. We agreed that it's best to research and write about a subject that is of interest to and is already somewhat understood by the writer. I mentioned that I knew something about the sweet corn canning industry in Northern New England (Maine, New Hampshire and Vermont), my family's farm adjoined a corn shop, and I had grown up producing sweet corn for processing in the shop. Canneries that can corn were referred to as corn factories, corn shops, canneries, vegetable canneries or canning plants. Although there is some regional differentiation (corn shop is largely found in Maine), for this story the terms are generally interchangeable.

Dr. Sauer's response was enthusiastic. He encouraged my investigation of the region's corn packing enterprises. As a long-

standing promoter of the importance of corn (maize) in understanding
American culture, there was no question that another portion of the
story should be examined.[2] Thus, this project was born. The discarded
topic was island sheep (sheep production on Maine's coastal islands).
But for that brief exchange, this reading adventure would likely be
about wool across waves rather than canning gold.

Although the early varieties of sweet corn were white, by the 1930's
yellow types had become popular. To watch the flow of corn through
a cannery was to fantasize the canning of gold, for significant profits
were made by corn shop owners.

In 1968 I completed a thesis "Historical Geography of the Northern
New England Sweet Corn Canning Industry," received a Master's of
Science degree and moved on without publishing any of the work.[3] An
occasional revisit to the research and a few oral presentations were
about all the attention given to the topic until 1999. Because time and
heightened awareness attend a long career of watching landscapes and
people, I sensed an inner desire to renew the quest to better comprehend
my corner of the world. Using the 1968 thesis as a launching pad, and
a half year sabbatical leave from teaching duties at the University of
Maine at Farmington, I expanded my original literature review, added
published and unpublished data, interviewed seventy-five former corn
shop workers, managers, owners and farmers, and conducted a survey
of the status of old cannery buildings. Much of this new material has
been presented at recent professional meetings; consequently this book
is the culmination of my study started long ago in that silent office.[4]

Northern New England

The rural economy of Maine, New Hampshire and Vermont has been
in constant transition since initial settlement by European people.
Periodic readjustments to new economic conditions are readily visible
in today's landscape. Abandoned farmsteads in various stages of decay,
discontinued country roads, neat stone walls running through second and
third growth forest, villages that have lost all service functions and
derelict industrial buildings (including corn shops) are persuasive
evidence of many modifications in the rural economy of the three
Northern New England states.

From the mid-seventeenth to the mid-nineteenth century, most of the area experienced population growth and economic expansion. With few exceptions this development was based on an agricultural economy of small family farms. Beginning about 1850, this trend was replaced by a slow but constant out-migration of rural people. Many of these New Englanders moved to Ohio, Illinois, and other western states that were more conducive to agriculture than the rocky, thin soils of New England. A large number of people relocated to growing industrial cities-Lowell, Massachusetts; Lewiston, Maine; and Manchester, New Hampshire. In addition to losing much of its market to western competition, this loss of agrarian workers tended to increase rural labor costs and restrict farm production to commodities that could compete with goods produced in other parts of the nation. First meat, grain and wool production went west, later to be followed by selected vegetables. Dairying, eggs, potatoes, blueberries, apples, maple syrup and truck garden products continued to hold their own against western competition. Until the mid 1900's, sweet corn for canning was among these latter items.

Landscapes of Food and Fiber Procurement

Canning gold played a significant role in the economy of Northern New England from the 1860's to the 1960's. The dynamics of the industry are associated with a complex group of forces. Local food processing is closely linked to agricultural geography, which has a variety of traditional research approaches; study of landscapes, regional identity, concern for resources, food systems and farm policy.[5] The early establishment of the industry in Northern New England resulted from a group of initial advantages enjoyed by the region. As western lands became settled, economic reorientation of market areas followed. Psychological, political, historical, technological, economic and agronomic patterns greatly influenced the pace of this change.[6] Over time the initial advantages of Northern New England were lost to other areas with different attractions and the industry abandoned the area.

Shifting fortunes of individual commodities such as cheese, rice or cattle are frequently the basis of defining rural regions and understanding their dynamics.[7] Regional agricultural systems that change over time offer another way of understanding transformation forces. These concentrate on political or economic settings; for example, those of the Canadian Maritime Provinces or a southern Piedmont County.[8] Concern about the shifting role of food and fiber production in the countryside represents yet another strategy taken by scholars. These address the urban-rural interface, villages or the farmer's views, as well as comprehensive national or international studies.[9]

Economic and social alterations take place on a landscape and each change has a visual impact. Individually, decisions and events usually have only slight influences on the character of what is seen. Exceptions would include major constructions, as a new airport, or removals as may be the case when the old canning factory burns. Over time the landscape is transformed. New technology, for example, big round bales of hay, may make a field appear full of bison from a distance at harvest time. Abandoned farm buildings, empty industrial structures and changing land use are there to be observed and examined. Sauer in his 1925 "The Morphology of Landscape" established well framed principles for understanding how physical and cultural landscapes change.[10] Many rural landscapes have been systematically analyzed, but additional research is needed before they can be fully understood and appreciated.[11]

The rise and fall of the sweet corn industry was accompanied by change in economic conditions, change that left relics on the landscape and memories in the minds of many. More than 130 towns in the three Northern New England states had corn shops at one point in time (Figure 1.1). The operations were often long-standing features of rural communities; however, in other cases their lives spanned only a few canning seasons. At the industry's peak, 1900-1930, more than a hundred shops were canning corn each fall, employing six to seven thousand workers. By 1929 acres in sweet corn exceeded 20,000. Although only about 13 percent of the region's farms included it in their operations that year, in some areas of concentration, such as Oxford County, Maine, nearly a third of the farmers grew corn for the local factories. Other vegetables, fruits and meats were sometimes canned; however, sweet corn was the mainstay at most shops.

The purpose of this book is to investigate the factors associated with the growth and decline of the sweet corn canning industry of Northern New England. The spatial distribution of the industry is examined from a historical viewpoint, with an analysis of the physical, economic, and cultural conditions that contributed to and resulted from change. How various developmental and declining stages of the industry influenced landscapes and people are also documented.

This Book

Globalization and regional change are inseparable.[12] Plant diffusion, changing diets, industrial and transportation technology, expanding and emerging world markets, and wars all may impact regional economies, people and landscapes. The unique character of place is shaped by these conditions as they interact with the physical environment.

This book examines the shifting forces that modified Northern New England's rural landscape and attempts to link local patterns with pervasive and powerful forces that initiate and drive transformation. The rise and decline of regional industries is a process of spatial diffusion, contraction and disappearance as waves of change flow across landscapes and through mental images of people inhabiting places.[13] In the case of a single enterprise, sweet corn canning, the struggle to survive demanded various strategies addressing internal and external challenges. Initially, Northern New England benefited from globalization and the industry expanded. Then it began to suffer from these forces and corn shops closed. The region's sweet corn canning business failed to adequately adjust to shifting conditions, which led to the industry's demise. The wave took a century to flow over Northern New England and left a fading aftermath still evident on the landscape and remembered by people who canned gold.

Following the introductory chapter, the Northern New England sweet corn canning industry is traced from the pre-canning antiquity of the plant through the establishment, growth and decline of the enterprise, and its impact on the citizens and landscapes of places that once had corn shops. The antiquity aspect, Chapter 2, draws from materials on the origin and diffusion of sweet corn as a food. Chapter 3, which is about the relation of the physical environment to sweet corn and the establishment of the industry, depends on work relating commercial sweet corn production to evapotranspiration, moisture index, and literature on early experimental food processing and agricultural innovations. Data for the period prior to 1879 are not readily available, therefore, detailed trends in the early years of the industry are difficult to identify. Chapter 4 examines an era of rapid growth between 1880 and 1930. By the late 1800's the United States Agricultural Census began to include selected statistics on sweet corn production and some

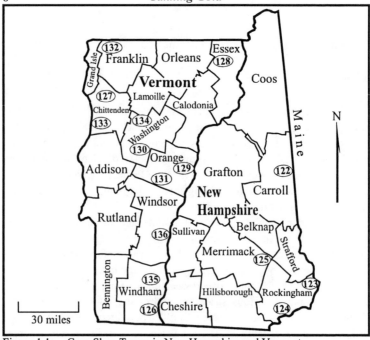

Figure 1.1a   Corn Shop Towns in New Hampshire and Vermont.

INDEX TO TOWNS

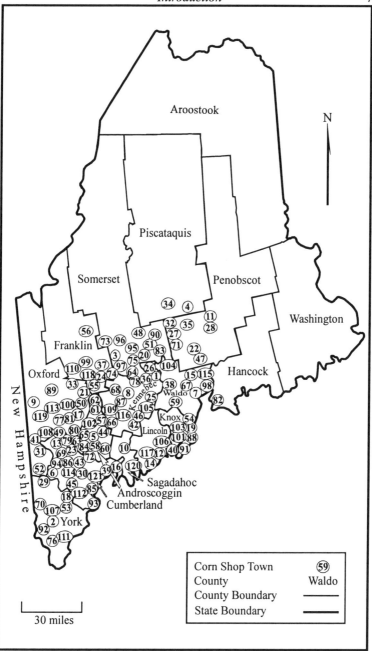

Figure 1.1b   Corn Shop Towns in Maine.

Sources for Figure 1.1: *Maine Register, State Year Book and Legislative Manual*
(Portland, Maine: Fred Tower Companies, 1873, 1880, 1890, 1910, 1920, 1930,
1940, 1950, 1960); *New Hampshire Register, State Year Book and Legislative
Manual* (Portland, Maine: Fred Tower Companies, 1910, 1920, 1930, 1940,
1950, 1960); *Walton's Register* (Vermont) *Business Directory, Almanac and
State Year Book* (Rutland, Vt.: The Tuttle Company, 1910, 1920); *Vermont Year
Book* (Chester, Vt.: National Survey Company, 1930, 1940, 1950, 1960)
information for 131 of the 136 corn shop towns is listed under "manufacturing"
in the above. Over the years municipal clerks were the most common reporters
of these materials; however, some were more timely and inclusive than others
in sending information to the register/year book editor. Additional
documentation for towns and/or corn canneries is from the following: Gleason
Ayres, "Business and Industry" in *History of Waterbury, Vermont: 1915-1991*
(Waterbury, Vt.: Waterbury Historical Society 1991, pp. 222-226); Randall H.
Bennett, *Bethel, Maine: A Illustrated History* (Bethel, Maine: Bethel Historical
Society, 1991); W. H. Bunting, *A Day's Work: A Sampler of Historic Maine
Photographs 1860-1920 Part Two* (Portland, Maine; Maine Preservation 2000);
Wesley Herwig, *Early Photographs of Randolph, Vermont 1855-1948* (Randolph
Center, Vt.: Greenhills Books, 1986); Janet M. Hounsell and Ruth B. D. Horne,
Conway, New Hampshire: 1765-1997 (Portsmouth, N.H.: Peter Randall
Publisher, 1998); *Bangor (Maine) Industrial Journal* various dates and years
from 1888 to 1918; Richard F. Talbot, "The Sweet Corn Industry in Maine,"
(bachelor's thesis, University of Maine, 1907). In some situations even owners
and town officials were confused about the locations of corn shops. Steve
Smith, "Corn Shop Days Remembered," *North Conway (N.H.) Reporter*, 20
January 1988, notes that H. C. Baxter Brothers Company built a cannery in
Lovell, Maine. Upon receipt of a higher than expected tax bill that could not be
resolved, the company dismantled the factory and reconstructed it just across the
generally recognized municipal boundary in neighboring Fryeburg, Maine. A
survey of the line revealed that the shop was still in Lovell. The Fryeburg
Town Clerk reported it in Fryeburg, which is what the owner intended. It
operated for only a few seasons before being dismantled a final time. For
purposes of this study, it is considered a Fryeburg corn shop. Despite an
extensive search of sources, it is possible that the author missed a few corn
shops and/or corn shop towns.

data on pack (cannery output) are published by the National Canners
Association. Spatial changes in the region's corn canning industry
indicate shifts in corn shop locations and production. Chapter 5, the
period of decline 1931 to 1968, relies extensively on detailed agricultural
and production statistics, published and unpublished materials, and

interviews with former farmers, owners, managers, and workers as well as my personal recall. Changes in sweet corn for processing location quotients illustrate the relative decline of the industry's importance in Northern New England compared to other producing areas.

Chapter 6 is an effort to understand the collective character of the corn shop towns, including people that grew and canned the product. Who were these people? How did the sweet corn endeavor shape communities and the folks that lived in them? What landscape relics remain from the industry? Interviews with former owners, managers, farmers and workers, and a survey of old corn cannery buildings or sites where they once stood provide a basis for profiling the people and places that once canned gold.

A concluding, Chapter 7 contains thoughts about relentless change that produces new opportunities followed by fading dreams and yet more innovation, additional opportunities and more change. A system that once brought hope, economic reward and social interaction was replaced by different expectations, possibilities and life-styles.

Canning gold in Northern New England ceased in 1968. Memories and landscape relics are both passing, but there is still time to capture them. Another assortment of canneries and the people that ran them are part of America's image of place.[14] Corn shops are not in a row, overlooking sunny Monterey Bay, but they contributed much to shaping another region 3,000 miles east of John Steinbeck's node. While visiting Cannery Row in 1981 and 1999, I observed the conversion of old smelly fish processing buildings into up-scale hotels and other tourist attractions. I have no such expectations for corn factories.

Chapter 2

Pre-Canning Antiquity of Sweet Corn

Historically, the term sweet corn has often been associated with any maize that is eaten while in the milk stage. There are six different types of corn (maize) that collectively are referred to as Indian corn; dent, flint, sweet, pop, flour and pod. Dent is characterized by a small depression in each kernel after it dries. Most corn grown in the U.S. is dent. Flint has smooth kernels when dried. It requires a shorter growing season than dent and will store longer without deterioration; but its yields are more modest. Both dent and flint are considered field corns because of the high percentage of each that is consumed as livestock feed. Various human foods and industrial products utilize the rest of the production. Sweet has a retarded sugar to starch conversion rate and most is eaten in its milk stage as a vegetable. Hard-skinned pop kernels burst when heat expands internal moisture. Flour is recognized by its soft kernels when ripe and is easy to grind by hand. It was popular with pre-industrial groups and is still grown in parts of South America. Pod has a separate covering over each individual kernel and is not grown for commercial use because pod removal is labor intensive.

Origin of Sweet Corn

During milk stage the sugar content of any corn is relatively high. The major difference between true sweet corn (*Zea mays sccharate*) and other maize varieties is that the former has a reduced ability to change its sugary endosperm into starch. Endosperm is the food supply stored within a seed that nourishes the seed's embryo as it develops to form a new plant.

George F. Carter, in his 1948 researh on sweet corn among the Indians, points out that:

> All other varieties of corn, ...pass through a sugary stage but convert their sugary endosperm into starch...Some field corns, such as the Corn Belt dents, make poor eating even picked at their best. Others, such as the *elotes* of some parts of Mexico, are probably as flavorful as our best sweet corn.[1]

The genetic characteristics of corn make for frequent mutations; thus, complex lineage is associated with each race.[2] Mandelsdorf notes there is general agreement among plant geneticists that true sweet corn is a mutation of field corn. Evidence indicates that this mutation may occur in both dent and flint corn, and he is convinced that genetic patterns in today's sweet corns can be traced to a single origin region, the highlands of Peru and Bolivia.[3] E.W. Lindstrom demonstrated that sweet corn could develop from a dent corn mutation. In 1929 he discovered a sweet corn kernel among a group of pedigree dent corns. After four generations of crossing with normal sweet corn, all proof indicated that the original kernel was a mutant from the dent corn.[4] Gerdes and Tracy note that most sweet corn germplasm is derived from Northern Flint corn. Midwest dents represent a genetic pool that may improve some varieties.[5] Germplasm is the substance in germ cells by which heredity characteristics are believed to be transmitted. Three major types of sweet corn are known; Andean sugar which is too starchy to be a true sweet corn, Mexican sugar which has both a relatively high sugar and starch content, and North American sugar which has a high percentage of sugar in its endosperm.[6] Sweet corn's family tree is complicated but the primary contributions to its gene pool have been traced.

Indian Use of Sweet Corn

There is a considerable amount of disagreement concerning the age of sweet corn. Because it is impossible to determine the exact time and place that the first sweet corn kernel developed, an examination of the historical use of the plant is helpful in determining its antiquity. Many of the early references concerning the usage of sweet corn make no distinction between true sweet corn and field corn in the milk stage; therefore, it is often difficult to know if the work is dealing with *Zea mays sccharata* or a field corn being used as a sugar corn.

Indian corn is a plant that probably cannot exist in a wild state. Alphonse DeCandolle concisely summarizes this widely accepted theory:

> ... maize is a plant singularly unprovided with means of dispersion and protection. The grains are hard to detach from the ear, which is itself enveloped. They have no tuft or wing to catch the wind, and when the ear is not gathered by man the grains fall still fixed in the receptacle, and then rodents and other animals must destroy them in quantities, and all the more that they are not sufficiently hard to pass through the digestive organs. Probably so unprotected a species was becoming extinct, when a wandering tribe of savages, having perceived its nutritious qualities saved it from destruction by cultivating it. [7]

In all likelihood, many generations passed between the time of maize domestication and the first intentional cultivation of sweet corn. The sugary character of the plant is easily recognized and it is genetically recessive; therefore, it is relatively simple to grow in a fairly pure form. Archaeological evidence that might reveal the age of *Zea mays sccharata* is limited. An ear of pre-Columbian sweet corn was discovered by Earl H. Morris in New Mexican Aztec ruins. Morris estimates that it was grown between A.D. 1200 and 1300. According to A.T. Erwin, "The wrinkled pericarp, translucent endosperm and character of the starch grain clearly identify it as sweet corn."[8] H. G. Alexander and Paul Reiter collected a single kernel of what appears to be true sweet corn from Jemez Cave, New Mexico, and E. F. Castetter and W. H. Bell identified a few grains of corn from Nitsie Canyon, Arizona, as sweet corn.[9] Both of these finds are estimated to have grown around A.D. 1300. After extensive research into archaeological evidence concerning the origin of sweet Indian corn, G. W. Hendry concludes that at least one mutation of sweet corn occurred prior to A.D. 1535 in the Peruvian highlands of South America.[10] The absence of any large scale discovery of pre-Columbian sweet corn suggests that the plant is of relatively recent origin. These few examples of pre-1492 sweet corn may have been local mutants that had no special significance. In addition to the rather weak archaeological data, linguistic evidence in support of the theory that sweet corn was an important food among American Indians is lacking. Erwin points out:

The tribes, however widely separated, had a common root for that important cereal (maize); thus, among the Delawares we find the term 'winaminge' the month of August, literally the time of roasting ears. This appellation applies equally well to field corn, a crop which is known to have been used for roasting ears by the Indians. So far as we have been able to learn, the equivalents to the term sweet corn or sugar corn have no common root among the Indians.[11]

Although true sweet corn in some form undoubtedly existed among Native Americans, it is difficult to determine its various uses. Carl Sauer notes that native communities in Mexico and Guatemala have a great diversity of corns, each with its own use in the family diet and in South America it was often prized as a green vegetable as well as a source of chicha (beer).[12] Corn that produced high quality chicha was especially treasured. Indians of Ecuador, Peru and Bolivia desired sugar corn that was used for making alcoholic drink and parched corn.[13] Sweet corn, or *Maiz Dulce* as it is known in Mexico, has never held an important role among the Indians of that nation. Wellhausen, Roberts and Hernandez X point out that, although sweet corn is apparently a long established plant in the country, "there is no direct evidence, archaeological or otherwise, of the antiquity of *Maiz Dulce* in Mexico..."[14] In a letter to A.T. Erwin, August 17, 1946, Edgar Anderson reports:

> Sweet corn is not grown for green corn. So far as is known, it is always grown for its sugary content and is used either in primitive sweet drinks or in primitive kinds of candy. Only at fiesta time, ... does it come into city markets...It is never thought of as being of any use as a table corn and one is nearly always told that it is too sticky for that purpose and will gum up the teeth.[15]

Kelley and Anderson report that sweet corn was known throughout the state of Jalisco although it was not a commercial plant.[16] Erwin believes that many sweet corn mutations probably occurred in Mexico. Because they were not utilized enough to justify cultivation and propagation, most of them quickly died out.[17] Tribes of the Upper Missouri River cultivated a type of maize that the early white travelers to that area referred to as sweet corn. George F. Will and George E. Hyde believe this so-called sweet corn was actually a common species of tender field corn which was harvested in the milk stage, but they also point out that some of the tribes had a true sweet corn that was allowed to ripen and then used to make corn balls.[18] John Witthoft, in his comprehensive inventory of green corn ceremonialism among Eastern Woodland Indians, found little references to the use of corn in its milk stage. The Cherokee of North Carolina (1818) appear to have placed significant value on milk corn of the new harvest.[19] Various Indian tribes of Northeastern United States may have possessed a true sweet corn at the time of the area's settlement by whites. According to an article by an individual identified as Plymotheus, appearing in the July 6, 1822 edition of the *Old Colony Memorial* of Plymouth, Massachusetts, sweet corn was cultivated by the Iroquois in the 1700's.[20] The exact usage of this crop among these Indians is not clear; there is some confusion as to whether or not sweet corn was intentionally propagated. Although true sweet corn mutated many times and was known to many tribes, it never became a significant food crop. In their work, *Corn Among the Indians of the Upper Missouri,* Will and Hyde identify one hundred and four varieties of corn from eighteen tribes scattered across the United States. Only six of these are classified as sweet corn. Twelve of the eighteen sample tribes did not have sweet corn.[21] In addition to limited uses of sweet corn, A.T. Erwin states:

> The tendency of sweet corn, under favorable environment..., to revert to field corn type of becoming more starchy or to form 'starch caps' is well recognized. Sweet corn is inherently a plant of less vigor and stamina than field corn...In view of these facts sweet corn mutations would be less likely to survive than field corn in the struggle for existence under the rugged environment of Indian agriculture.[22]

Sweet Corn: A New England Domestication?

In his 1942 article on the origin of sweet corn, Erwin argues that true sweet corn is a post-Columbian plant developed from field corn mutations by white settlers of New England during the early 1800's.[23] Although Indians had sweet corn, evidence supports (1) that the first widespread use of the plant came among New England settlers and (2) most of the early sweet corn literature originates in this area. The article by Plymotheus states that sweet corn was introduced into Plymouth in 1779 from the Iroquois tribe.[24] In his "Sweet Corn-Mutant or Historic Species?" A.T. Erwin points out that the corn grown by

Plymotheus in 1822 probably is not the same as that introduced in 1779.

> It is difficult to maintain a pure strain of sweet corn wherever field corn
> is grown extensively even when isolated... Plymotheus reports this same
> difficulty for he states that in a few years it tended to lose 'much of its
> peculiar qualities of softness and sweetness... This corn grown by
> Plymotheus was undoubtedly sweet corn. If his seed did not come from
> the Iroquois, what was its source?   ...Could it not have been an
> unrecognized mutation originating at hand? The red cob which
> Plymotheus mentions, typical of newly developed mutations of dent corn,
> is highly suggestive of its recent origin.[25]

Thomas Jefferson's *Garden Book* of 1810 refers to shriveled corn, which
Erwin believes is sweet corn.[26] The source of this plant is not indicated.
In the *1821 Travel Letters of Timothy Dwight*, maize called sweet corn
is referred to as the most delicious vegetable of any known in this
country (New Haven, Connecticut).[27] This statement by Dwight
indicates sweet corn had been cultivated in the area for some time prior
to 1821. The first appearance of sweet corn in a seed catalogue came
in 1828. *Thorburn's Seed Catalogue* carried "sugar or sweet corn" that
year, and in 1838 the Massachusetts Horticultural Society offered
a prize for boiling corn.[28]

Sweet corn is a mutant of field corn that has lost much of its ability
to convert sugar into starch. Since the origin of maize this type of
mutation has occurred many times in widely scattered parts of America.
Some sweet mutants were utilized as a source of sugar by Native
people, but in general the restricted number of uses and the ecological
weakness of these plants gave sweet corn an insignificant role in Indian
agriculture. The first widespread propagation of the plant occurred
during the early 1800's in New England, where it was adopted as a
vegetable. By 1838 sweet corn had gained a popular position in the diet
of New Englanders. The demand for this food continued to increase and
with it the desire for preserving the flavor of fresh sweet corn.

Chapter 3

Birth of the Industry, 1840-1879

The sweet corn canning industry arose in Northern New England as a result of people's food habits, the physical environment, and the technological ability of businessmen and farmers. Sweet corn was well established in the diet of New Englanders by the late 1830's.

Physical Environment

Physical conditions within the New England states allowed for the production of many early sweet corn varieties. Most research on corn and the natural environment has focused on the various field corns. Certain aspects of field corn investigation also apply to sweet corn, but because the latter is used in its milk stage rather than in the ripe stage, the ecological balance is considerably different from that of grain corn.

Relationship of Sweet Corn to The Physical Environment

Previous research into climatic conditions that affect sweet corn growth has been based, for the most part, on the accumulation of heat units and the rainfall between the last killing frost in the spring and the first one in the fall. This concept of accumulating energy was first introduced in 1918.[1] According to this system:

> Degree-hour summations...were based on the hypothesis that for the production of crops a certain number of degree-hours above the zero point, which for corn is 49°F, are merely added. Because it is possible to determine from previous records the number of degree-hours required to

mature any variety of corn, the progress of the crop can be readily determined at any given moment from recording thermograph charts, provided, of course, the date of planting is known.[2]

Degree-days are converted into heat-units by omitting the twenty-four hour multiplier. Huelsen points out that heat summations are fairly accurate under conditions where air temperature alone is the controlling growth factor. It is not reliable where soil moisture, fertility, disease, insects and other environmental facts act as variables. Excessively low or high temperatures will also cause the system to be unreliable.[3] The number of heat-units required by the different varieties of sweet corn differs considerably (Table 3.1).

Hybrid	Total Heat Units For Fancy Whole Kernal Maturity
Gold Rush	1,520 - 1,580
Golden Bantam	1,675 - 1,735
Tendermost	1,800 - 1,860
Country Gentleman	1,990 - 2,050

Table 3.1   Heat Unit Requirements for Selected Varieties of Sweet Corn. *Source*: Huelsen, *Sweet Corn,* p. 240.

In addition to energy, available moisture is of major significance to the growth and development of sweet corn, or any other plant. Precipitation data give some indication of the amount of moisture that may be utilized by the vegetation, but do not take into account soil moisture and changing rates of evapotranspiration.

Each plant has a direct relationship to both the climatic moisture index and the potential evapotranspiration of its local environment. These two factors indicate with considerable accuracy the climatic conditions of any given area. Potential evapotranspiration is the theoretical amount of water that can be lost through evaporation and transpiration. Actual evapotranspiration is the amount of water that is lost through evaporation and transpiration. Potential evapotranspiration is useful because it is "...essentially determined by available energy and is, for all practical purposes, independent of vegetation, soil, or precipitation.[4]

Various moisture index systems have been developed. In 1948, C. W. Thornthwaite established an index that used a zero value where moisture adequacy and deficiency were compensatory. The region of prevailing sufficient moisture is separated from the region of persistently inadequate moisture. Thornthwaite's system consisted of an index of humidity, ratio of water surplus (sum for the months when precipitation exceeded soil moisture storage opportunity, and current potential evapotranspiration) to potential evapotranspiration, and an aridity index or ratio of water deficit (sum for all of the months in which potential evapotranspiration is theoretically larger than precipitation plus the amount of moisture that could be removed from soil moisture storage) to potential evapotranspiration.[5] In 1955 a method was developed to account for the decreasing supply of capillary moisture as soil dries. It was agreed upon that moisture deficit can begin as soon as any moisture is evapotranspired from the soil. Under this system the moisture index of any given location is arrived at in the following manner.

$$\text{Moisture Index} = \text{Humidity Index} - \text{Aridity Index}$$

$$= \frac{\text{Surplus}}{\text{PE}} \quad - \quad \frac{\text{Deficit}}{\text{PE}}$$

Because surplus equals precipitation minus the actual evapotranspiration, provided there is no change in storage and deficit is the difference between the actual and potential evapotranspiration, the moisture index formula is reduced to:

$$\text{Moisture Index} = 100 \left(\frac{\text{Precipitation}}{\text{Potential Evapotranspiration}} \right) -1$$

Moisture holding capacity differs greatly among the various soil types; thus areas with similar climatic conditions may have slightly different moisture indices.[6]

Sweet corn is able to grow under a wide range of climatic conditions. Commercial production of sweet corn is usually in areas that have a potential evapotranspiration of 490 to 800 millimeters [19.3 to 31.5 inches] (Figure. 3.1). The natural moisture index is not so critical as the potential evapotranspiration, because by irrigation the actual evapotranspiration of an area is artificially increased. Canneries which rely primarily on non-irrigated sweet corn are between 15 and 55 on the moisture index scale. Although in some dry years even normally humid areas may need irrigation, the most extensive irrigation sweet corn agriculture is carried on in those areas where the moisture index is near or below zero. Abandoned canning factories of Northern New England are, for the most part, on the low potential evapotranspiration, high moisture index fringe. Two sweet corn antiquity sites fall within the same general range of potential evapotranspiration as the commercial canning establishments of 1967. Jalisco's early sites fall within areas of artificial actual evapotranspiration. For comparison, several stations within the American Corn Belt have been plotted. Using these examples as indicators, field corn exhibits a noticeable tendency to prosper in areas with greater potential evapotranspiration and smaller moisture index than most sweet corn varieties. The exact relationship between any crop and the potential evapotranspiration-moisture index is difficult to pinpoint, but the general climatic boundary of commercial production of the sweet corn is delimited.

Sweet corn thrives in a variety of soil conditions. Victor Boswell evaluates ideal sweet corn producing soil:

> ...optimum ph is 5.5 to 7.0. Sweet corn is moderately tolerant to high salt and to high boron content of the soil. It grows well on any well drained soil that produces good yields of other crops. Deep, naturally rich soils that are easy to work are preferred but not essential. Sweet corn requires relatively heavy manuring and fertilizing of soils that are not naturally highly fertile. Fine sandy loams and sandy loams are best for crops for early markets; loams, silt loams, clay loams and clays can be used for later crops.[7]

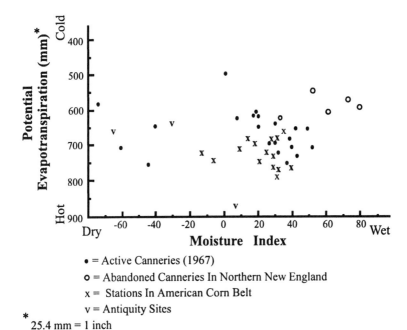

• = Active Canneries (1967)

o = Abandoned Canneries In Northern New England

x = Stations In American Corn Belt

v = Antiquity Sites

* 25.4 mm = 1 inch

Figure 3.1   Relationships Between Climatic Moisture Index, Potential Evapo-transpiration and Sweet Corn in the United States and Mexico. *Source:* Author; Data from Average Climatic Water Balance Data of the Continents, Part VII United States," *Publications in Climatology,* XVII, No. 3 (1964), pp. 456-615; Only Mexican site plotted from "Average Climatic Water Balance Data of the Continents, Part VI North America (Excluding United States)." *Publications in Climatology,* XVII, No. 2 (1964), p. 381; Stations and data are recorded in Appendix A.

Physical Environment of Northern New England

Whether or not sweet corn is grown for commercial canning in Northern New England depends to a large extent upon economic competition from other parts of the United States. Measured by heat units, Maine, New Hampshire and Vermont can produce earlier sweet corns such as Gold Rush and Golden Bantam (Table 3.2). The only heat-units that influence the growth of a plant are those during the growing season. The growing season is the length of time between the last killing frost in the spring and the first killing frost in the fall.

Location	Heat Units
Concord, New Hampshire	1,673
Lewiston, Maine	1,778
Burlington, Vermont	1,825

Table 3.2   Heat Unit Accumulation for Selected Northern New England Locations. *Source:* R.M. Bailey, et. al., *A Regional Approach to Breeding and Testing of Sweet Corn in the Northeast,* Agricultural Experiment Station Bulletin 704, University Park, Pa., Pennsylvania State University, 1963.

Northern New England's growing season is somewhat shorter than those of the Middle Atlantic and Midwest areas (Figure 3.2). As would be expected, the average growing season of the sweet corn areas of Maine, New Hampshire and Vermont is perfectly safe for the crop. It is the exceptional year that causes trouble. Late spring freezes or early fall frosts may shorten the length of the growing season as much as a month. Years with short growing seasons lead to low sweet corn yields and economic loss to both farmers and canners. The abandoned Northern New England corn canning factories are on the margin of commercial sweet corn production (Figure 3.1). The one Northern New England plant that operated in 1967 was functioning under these same general climatic conditions. This shift of commercial sweet corn canning to slightly warmer and drier climates may reflect increased use of hybrid sweet corn that is better adapted to a greater potential evapotranspiration and lower moisture index than Northern New England offers. At the critical milk stage when sweet corn is processed, potential evapotranspiration plays a major role in the length of time that the crop is in its best edible stage. For the most part, work dealing with sugar content of sweet corn and canning quality has been associated with temperature. There is an association between location and length of time that sweet corn is in the best edible stage (Table 3.3). The time of suitable quality sweet corn lasts about 2.5 days in Charleston, South Carolina, whereas it gets progressively longer as more northern stations are examined. Carlson and Weston feel:

In the Southern states where the temperature is comparatively high at picking time the corn remains in the best edible stage only two or three days. In Maine, however, where the corn is picked during the cool autumn period the corn remains in the best canning stage for four or five days. Because of the cool weather in Maine at picking time, it is easier to get the corn to the factory in prime condition than it is in the states farther south. This is one reason for the high quality of Maine sweet corn.[8]

Location Season	Picking		Length of Time In Best Edible State
Charleston, SC	June	17-31	2.5 days
	July	1-15	2.0 days
Baltimore, MD	August	1-15	2.5 days
	August	16-31	3.0 days
New Haven, CT	August	1-15	3.0 days
	August	16-31	3.5 days
Portland, ME	September	1-15	4.5 days
	September	16-30	5.5 days

Table 3.3   Length of Time Sweet Corn is in its Prime Edible Condition at Selected Locations. *Source*: Karl Sax, *Sweet Corn Breeding Experiments,* Maine Agricultural Experiment Station Bulletin #332 (Orono, ME,: University of Maine, 1926), p. 139.

The influence of moisture upon the development of sweet corn at the prime edible stage is not indicated in Sax's study at the University of Maine. Corn in the milk stage has a high water content which suggests the importance of humidity. According to Carlson and Weston, at an average temperature of 60°F sweet corn remains in satisfactory canning condition for five days.[9] No moisture control was considered in this temperature research. In their 1926 study Magoon and Culpepper found that:

Of seasonal factors concerned with growing and canning of sweet corn, temperature was found to be the most important as affecting the quality of the canned product. The rainfall had a very marked effect upon the vegetative activities of the plant, but produced no significant effect on the chemical composition of the cut corn or the quality of the canned product.[10]

Soils of eastern, central and southern Maine, southern New Hampshire, and eastern and western Vermont were able to support the commercial production of several sweet corn varieties. The climatic conditions of northern and eastern Maine, and the mountain regions of

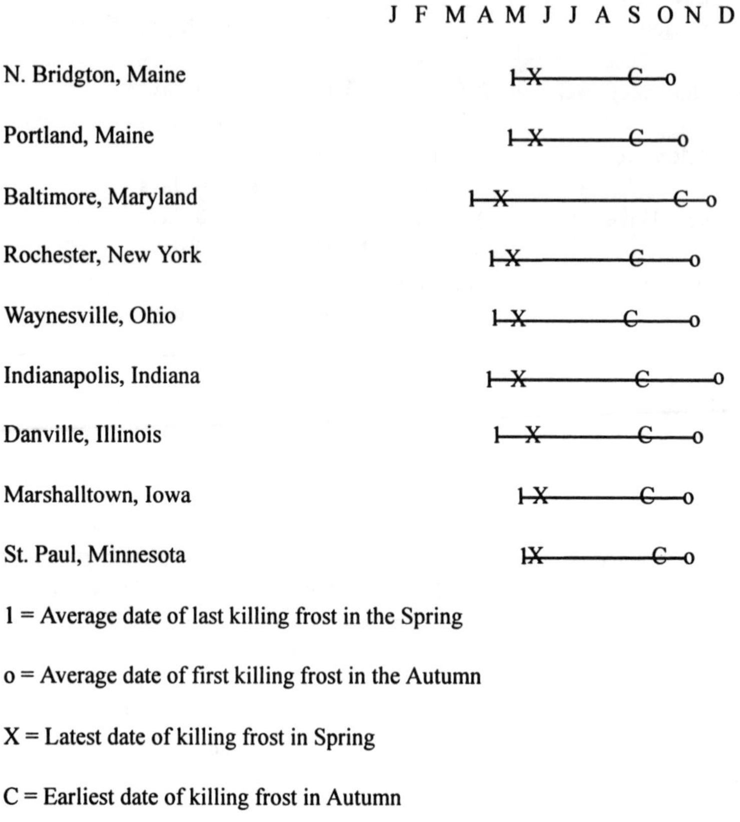

	J F M A M J J A S O N D
N. Bridgton, Maine	l—X C—o
Portland, Maine	l—X C—o
Baltimore, Maryland	l—X C—o
Rochester, New York	l—X C—o
Waynesville, Ohio	l—X C—o
Indianapolis, Indiana	l—X C—o
Danville, Illinois	l—X C—o
Marshalltown, Iowa	l—X C—o
St. Paul, Minnesota	lX C—o

l = Average date of last killing frost in the Spring

o = Average date of first killing frost in the Autumn

X = Latest date of killing frost in Spring

C = Earliest date of killing frost in Autumn

Figure 3.2   Growing Seasons for Selected Locations in Eastern and Midwestern United States. *Source:* Adapted from Carlson and Weston 1934, p. 391.

New Hampshire and Vermont, retard the crop. Stony and gravelly loams make up most of the soils within the sweet corn producing areas. An exception is the Lake Champlain Basin which is composed primarily of clays and silts (Fig. 3.3). All of these soils are somewhat acidic and usually deficient in lime and phosphorus. Surface horizons of these soils have a high organic content, but because of large amounts of acids and nutrients held in organic form they are released slowly for plant growth.[11] Pockets of relatively fertile alluvial soils exist in narrow river valleys throughout Northern New England, but in general they require substantial amounts of fertilizer for commercial production.[12]

The processes involved in maturing corn seed drain heavily upon the soil, but because sweet corn is harvested in the milk stage, it removes considerably fewer nutrients from the soil than grain corn.[13] The Northern New England soils are better adapted to sweet corn, which draw relatively few chemicals from the earth than they are for those crops that remove great amounts of nourishment.

In addition to climate and soil conditions, topography influences the commercial production of sweet corn. Because the wide spacing of corn plants permits little soil to be held by the root system, erosion may become a significant problem where corn fields have excessive slope. Areas with very little or no slope, provided they are well drained, are more suitable for the production of sweet corn.

Origin of Sweet Corn Canning

Industries are created in response to demand for new products and innovations to produce them. Food acquisition and consumption patterns were transformed during the mid-nineteenth century. Investors and innovators led the way with farmers and laborers happy to see opportunities for a cash crop or a wage. Canned goods, including corn, became standard dietary fare.

Markets

Market forces tend to drive technology, and sweet corn canning fits nicely into that framework. War, exploration, travel and potential mass consumption by the general public are the traditional motivators. During the period from 1790 to 1870 two major conflicts, the Napoleonic Wars in Europe and the Civil War in the U.S., placed great

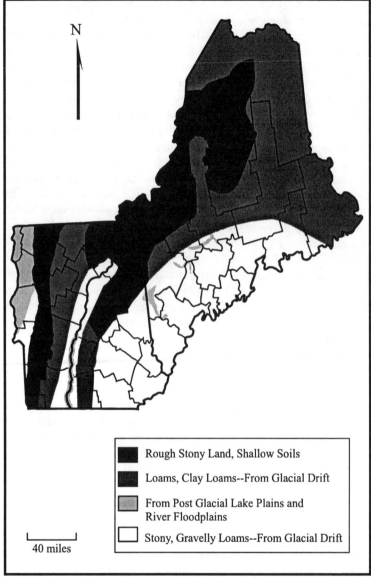

Figure 3.3   Major Soil Regions of Northern New England. *Source:* Adapted from Brady, Struchtemeyer and Musgrave, p. 600.

pressure on food suppliers to preserve products for troops. The long haul sailing industry generated demand for food stuffs with extended shelf-lives as did the ever moving western frontier. Exploding urban growth also represented an outlet for canned goods.

The practice of preserving food in hermetically sealed containers evolved during the late 1700's and early 1800's. Nicholas Appert is credited with this invention, which transformed the market for perishable goods from a radius of a few miles to, theoretically, the entire world. Documentation is rather spotty, but it is generally agreed that Ezra Daggett brought the canning secret to the United States between 1815 and 1818. He joined with Thomas Kensett to establish the first American canning enterprise. By 1819 this firm was packing salmon and lobsters for sale to the public. William Underwood and Company began to process hermetically preserved foods in 1822.[14] The early canning enterprises were concerned primarily with experimentation and were rather limited in size.

The general principles of canning food were well known before efforts began with sweet corn. Isaac Winslow, who visited France and possibly learned the art of canning while there, is the founder of the corn canning industry.[15] After retiring from the sea in 1839, Winslow settled in Portland, Maine, and devoted much of his time to perfecting a process to preserve sweet corn in hermetically sealed containers. His first cans were constructed from short sections of ordinary water spout with each end closed. The can with contents was cooked over a fire, a hole punched to let out steam and then the small opening was soldered over. Edward Lamb another Portland tinner invented the processing of soldering caps on cans.[16] The earliest attempts to can corn were made with kernels attached to the cob, but this method met with repeated failure. Finally in 1844, after removing the kernels from the cob, Winslow proved that green corn, after being subjected to a specific degree of heat for a certain length of time, would retain its natural flavor for an indefinite period.[17] Records of Winslow's business activities are not very definite. The earliest report of "Winslow's" corn being sold on an urban market is an invoice dated February 19th, 1848 for one dozen canisters of preserved corn to Samuel S. Pierce of Boston, Massachusetts, for the price of four dollars.[18] As a man who understood the difficult task of preserving food on long sea voyages, he recognized the potential market for canned goods in the sailing industry.

A seaport was an ideal location to promote canning. As is often the case, innovators are motivated by a desire to impress peers as much as by fiscal gain. Winslow's brother, Hezekial, who continued to captain ships, would take a supply of canned corn on board and share it with other shippers he met in foreign ports or at sea.[19] What a marketing agent! Soon Winslow's firm had sales offices in San Francisco and Australia.[20] This business continued under the direction of Isaac Winslow and operated in the tin and stove shop of his brother, Nathan, on Front Street in Portland, Maine. Nathan, an unofficial partner of Isaac, joined the business in 1852 and soon John Winslow Jones, Isaac's nephew, became a partner.[21] Following success in processing corn, they constructed two corn shops in the early 1850's, one in the Riverton section of Portland and a second in nearby Gorham.[22] This three-man partnership continued until 1862, at which time Jones took control of the company. The large extended Winslow/Jones family provided both working capital and business links that were critical in the start-up of a new experimental enterprise. A sister and brother-in-law provided a supply of vegetables from their farm for trial canning.[23] In addition to John Winslow Jones, two other sizeable corn canning companies arose in Northern New England during this early era. Samuel Rumery became associated with sweet corn canning in 1845. In the late 1850's he joined with George Burnham Jr., in the canning business. James P. Baxter became a leading member of the Rumery and Burnham Company in 1862. This organization split to form two businesses. Rumery, Baxter and William Davis established the Portland Packing Company while Burnham and Charles Morrill started the Burnham & Morrill Company.[24] These three companies, J. Winslow Jones, Portland Packing and Burnham & Morrill benefited greatly from supply contracts with the Union Army and dominated the Northern New England corn canning industry during the years following the Civil War. Each of these concerns established its head office at Portland, Maine, and that city became the region's corn canning hub. Data dealing with the location and production of canning plants before 1880 are limited. According to Clarence A. Day, in 1868 J. Winslow Jones owned five canneries, two were located at Westbrook, while Bridgton, Yarmouth and Fairfield each had one. Jones had contracted farmers for about two thousand acres of sweet corn at the price of five cents per quart of corn removed from the cob.[25] The first comprehensive report of canning establishments in a Northern New England state appeared in the 1873 edition of *The Wealth and Industry of Maine*. Thirteen plants were processing hermetically sealed vegetables, primarily corn. J. Winslow Jones operated factories in Bridgton, Deering (now part of Portland), Farmington, and Fairfield; Portland Packing processed at Casco, Cumberland, Deering, Gorham, Naples, and Windham; and Burnham & Morrill had establishments in Minot, Paris, and Scarboro (Scarborough) (Figure. 3.4 a).[26]

The factory at Farmington is representative of locations most desired. It had been built to take advantage of fertile bottomland along the Sandy River, which was to become a major sweet corn area (Figure 3.5). The village assurred a supply of labor. Rail service was available. Nearness to the Sandy River guaranteed water for steam, cooling, and flushing liquid waste, which was carried away by the river. Husks and cobs were used by local farmers for cattle feed. Water that went into the cans came from more sanitary sources, such as wells. However, flooding was a problem.

A State of Maine statistician estimated that in 1873 Maine's plants processed 5,700,000 cans of sweet corn along with 900,000 cans of succotash and shell beans.[27] The can sizes utilized in these packs are not given, therefore, it is impossible to determine the exact size or value of the industry's output. Although, sweet corn was the leading product of these companies, other vegetables, fruits, and seafood items were also packed.

Canning Innovations

The corn canning process in the 1860's and 70's involved many steps. The raw product arrived at the factory and was deposited in an open shed by the farmer. Crews would hand husk each ear. Then the ears would be inspected for insects and damage with all unacceptable corn being cut from the ear. They were then washed to remove silk and dirt. Cutters then cut the kernels from each ear. Syrup (sugar, salt and starch) to flavor and provide specific consistency was mixed into the corn. Cooking took place for a period and then the product was placed in hand-made tin cans, and caps to close the fill holes were soldered in place. More cooking was required. After additional cooking, a hole in the caps that allowed steam to escape during the second cooking was closed with a single drop of solder. The cans were cooled in a water bath and placed in storage to await labels and shipping.[28]

During the years between 1840 and 1879 many innovations were in-

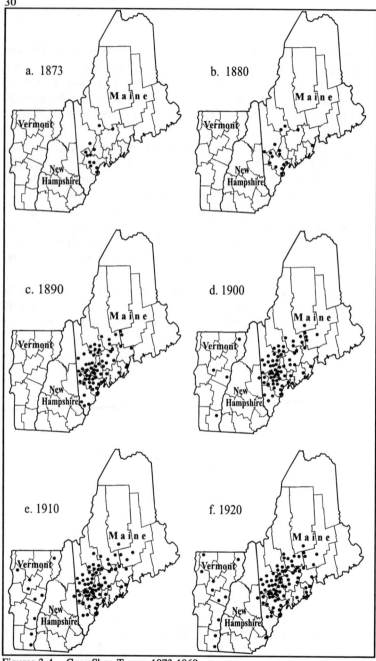

Figures 3.4   Corn Shop Towns, 1873-1968.

31

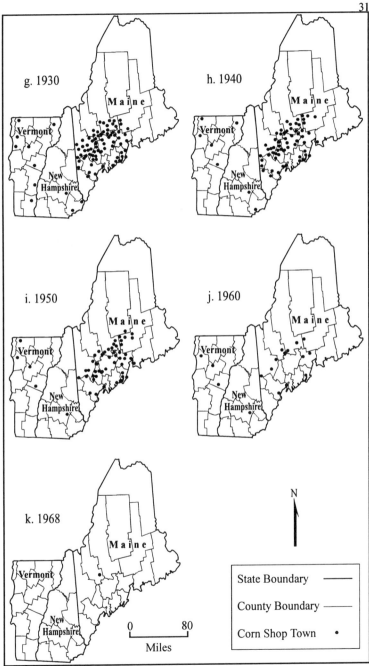

Source: See Figure 1.1

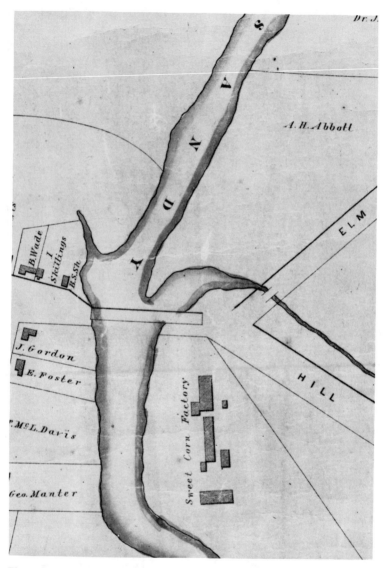

Figure 3.5   Sweet Corn Factory in Farmington, Maine, 1874. *Source*: E. F. Sanford, and C. T. Peggett, 1874. *Map of Farmington*, Maine, Philadelphia, Pa.: F. Bourguin.

troduced into the corn canning industry. The earliest of these arose in Maine, but as sweet corn processing spread south and west, so did the origin of corn canning innovations. Many of these new inventions applied to the overall canning industry, whereas, others were associated especially with sweet corn. Glass jars were often used in the early stages of hermetic processing, but because of the high breakage rate tin containers were increasingly used. The first of these cans were hand-made and often failed to preserve the contents.

> The methods of can making were for many years very slow and primitive. A tinner who could turn out sixty cans a day was a master workman...The body of each (can) had to be measured, marked and cut out from a plate by hand shears; to make the seam or top secure and air tight, it was thought necessary to pile on the solder until a ridge an eighth of an inch thick was built up from end to end. It was also a slow and difficult operation to make the corners and bottoms. Each one had first to be drawn on the tin with compass and then cut out with shears, and finally with a mallet the edge struck up or bent over an upright piece of iron called "a heading stake." The tops and bottoms, like the seams, were soldered on with a heavy beading of metal...[29]

The invention of a machine to stamp out can bodies and covers by Thomas Kensett in 1847 greatly reduced the amount of labor required in can production. Once the pre-cut tin can had been perfected, canners felt that the most significant labor step was hand capping the full cans. Huelsen reports that, "a good capper was the highest paid worker on the payroll. Strikes were frequent, and the canner was at the mercy of the boss capper."[30]

The first application for a patent directly associated with corn canning came in 1853 when Isaac Winslow asked to be granted one for the preservation of green corn. This was not approved until 1862 at which time John Winslow Jones received the rights to all his uncle's innovations.[31] Some corn canning patents resulted in lawsuits. One of the industry's most bitter patent disputes occurred this way:

> Jones attempted to collect royalties on the patents and started suit against the estate of Henry Clark of Wiscasset, Maine, in 1867. The suit was decided in favor of Jones in 1873. Other canners agreed to pay Jones a royalty of 25 cents a dozen cans until 1878 when the patents expired. However, the case was appealed and in October, 1875, the U.S. Supreme

Court reversed the decision.[32]

Because a few of the processing patents included aspects of fish packing, the court decisions influenced a sphere much larger than the corn canning industry.[33] These controversial patents involved the cold pack canning process. Under this process the vegetable was cold packed in the can, sealed, and then cooked in boiling water for two hours. The cans were then vented and resealed followed by a period of two and a half to three hours longer in boiling water ... the process time was gradually reduced as the practice of adding salts to the water bath became more general.[34] Jones revised his patents and received control of an improved corn knife and mechanical corn cutter in 1876.[35] These patents, which brought him royalties from corn canners throughout the United States along with his expanding canning industry, placed J. Winslow Jones in the lead among Northern New England food processing interests.

Although a crude retort had been developed by Appert in France in 1852, the cold pack method dominated corn canning until G. Lewis Merrell and Oscar F. Soule of Syracuse, New York, perfected a process in which cans were filled, hermetically sealed and placed in a steam tight chamber. By confining the steam within the chamber, temperatures of 240° F. could be attained without danger of destroying the tin cans.[36] This hot pack process did not play a significant role in corn canning until about 1879.

In addition to developing a reliable tin can and an efficient method of cooking, which applied to all types of canning, the sweet corn industry devoted a considerable amount of effort to the perfection of a rapid means of removing kernels from the cob. Two techniques were developed for the removal of kernels. Cream (Maine) style results when the corn is either scraped or cut from the cob in such a manner as not to detach the base of the kernel. Whole kernel (Maryland) style is the removal of the entire kernel by making the cut next to the cob. Maine style was the most popular in Northern New England during the 1800's. Various shaped hand knives had been invented, but none were fast enough to meet the demands of the canners. Huelsen points out that:

> In 1869 cutting was the most time-consuming task at a factory at Bridgton, Maine; of 800 hands employed, 300 were cutters and 100 huskers. This situation continued until 1875 when the first hand powered

cutter was introduced, the invention of Volney Barker of Denmark, Maine. One man and a boy could cut about 3000 pounds of ears in 10 working hours with this cutter.[37]

As a result of this and several lesser inventions associated with sweet corn processing, many consider Barker one of the most important men in early corn canning.

Plant Breeding Innovations

Sweet corn producers and canners devoted some time and effort to the improvement of both yield and quality of the crop. According to Karl Sax, sweet corn quality was based on the proportion of sugar and starch, the amount of crude fiber in the kernels, the number of rows of kernels and the whiteness of the corn. Sweet corn with large row numbers has small kernels which are desirable in canning cream style corn.[38] The significance of hybrid sweet corn was not realized by most canners and farmers during the middle of the nineteenth century, although there is evidence of serious experimentation along this line beginning in the 1820's. Hybrid sweet corn programs consist of two basic stages. After several generations of self pollination of individual plants, most undesirable characteristics are eliminated and a series of nearly uniform strains are created. However, during this process the vigor of the original sweet corn is lost. In order to regain its strength, the better of the inbred plants are hybridized. According to Hedricks:

> The improvement of sweet corn by hybridization seems to have started in the 1820's by Dr. Gideon B. Smith, who named one of the hybrids Early White. In a letter in the *Albany Cultivator* 1838, Dr. Smith wrote that Early White was a hybrid of two Indian corns, Tuscarora and Sioux, from crosses made ten or twelve years earlier. It is evident from Dr. Smith's letter that the hybridization of corn was well understood by him, ...yet, so unimportant was sweet corn, there seems to have been no other hybridizer who put his work on record after Dr. Smith, until 1850, when Reverend A. R. Pope, Somerville, Massachusetts, gave an account of breeding corn in *The Magazine of Horticulture*, December, 1850. His first hybrids were made in 1845, and sometime between that date and 1850 he named one of his crosses Old Colony, the first variety of this vegetable to receive general recognition by seedmen and gardeners;...[39]

With these exceptions nearly all of the sweet corn grown between 1839 and 1879 were non-hybrid varieties. Stowell's Evergreen arose in the 1850's as one of the more popular varieties. This was perfected by Nathan Stowell of Burlington, New Jersey, in 1850. It is a cross between a northern sugar corn and Memomony, a soft field corn. Stowell named it Stowell's Sweet Corn, but later changed this to Stowell's Evergreen.[40] Interest in Stowell's sweet corn is indicated in the *Working Farmer*, 1850. Editor Mapes reported that:

> ...if the stalks were placed in a cool dry place...the grains would remain full and milky for many months. Also the ears might be pulled in August and, by tying a string loosely around the small end to prevent the husks from drying away from the ear, they might be laid away on shelves and kept moist and suitable for boiling.[41]

This is the earliest reference to preserving sweet corn for boiling. Crosby was the most important canning variety in Northern New England during the years following the War Between the States. Josiah Crosby of Arlington, Massachusetts, developed it from an unknown cross about 1860. Another widely used variety of the 1870's was Moore's Concord, an 1865 cross of Crosby's Early and Burr's Improved.[42] Most of the sweet corn of this era was white, although there was considerable variation from one variety to another in terms of flavor.

Agricultural Innovations

Farmers that were contracted to grow sweet corn for the canneries also adapted innovations during the middle 1800's. The metal plow and other tilling implements aided farmers in crop production. Although developed primarily for planting field corn, the corn planter was certainly used in the sweet corn business. In their *History of Agriculture in the Northern United States 1620-1860*, Bidwell and Falconer point out that:

> In 1840 corn was dropped by hand and covered with the hoe or plow... During the fifties many new machines, much improved, came into use, some of which dropped both seed and fertilizer and covered and rolled them as fast as a horse could walk. It was claimed (in 1856) that the Billings machine, which had the essentials of a modern planter, was

capable of planting from 6 to 10 acres per day...Brown's Corn Planter was a double machine drawn by two horses, planting two rows at a time..."This machine" wrote one in 1861, "will plant 12 to 20 acres in a day and do the work better than a man can plant half an acre with a hoe."[43]

By 1879 various styles of corn planters were in widespread use throughout the corn growing areas of the United States.

Farmers

The quality and yield of the sweet corn crop depended not only upon the physical environments, seed variety, and mechanical innovations, but also on horticultural practices of individual contractors.   An early example of a sweet corn growing incentive appears in *The Maine Farmer:*

> In 1868, Ira Cisby, of South Paris, received the prize of $30 offered by Burnham and Morrill for the best acre of sweet corn grown for their factory that year. His acre yielded 2,635 cans of corn for which he received $118.12.[44]

Demand for sweet corn resulted in significant profits for growers and the chance to raise a new cash crop was always welcomed by farmers. By the 1870's experience with the crop had convinced many farmers to try sweet corn if they were within reasonable hauling distance of a cannery. As more cornshops were constructed, the number of potential growers increased. Hauling distance from farm to factory could be up to twelve miles, but that would be a marginal situation. Six miles was a more common limit. Farm profits from an acre of sweet corn exceeded those of field corn and this knowledge was widely disseminated by farm organizations such as the Grange and at public gatherings. Because sweet corn is a labor intensive crop, acreage on individual farms was often only an acre or less.[45]

Labor

As noted in the Bridgton factory (p. 34) corn shops needed large labor forces. The short canning season of only four to six weeks meant that most of the workers had to be drawn from the unemployed, underemployed or people that could take time from a full-time job. During this period many of the tasks such as husking and cutting were done by hand and were not considered skilled. Housewives, lumbermen, farm help, children and the infirm were considered good help. Even into the 1950's one corn cannery employee who wished to remain anonymous, remarked that the shop was run by housewives, drunks and disabled people.[46] This opportunity for wage jobs, although seasonal, had strong appeal to rural women. Until this time most who wished to find employment for a paycheck had to depart home for milltowns, such as Lowell, Massachusetts and Lewiston, Maine.[47] The role of children in the fruit and vegetable canning business was extensive. In 1879 children represented eighteen percent of the labor force in the industry (Table 3.4). Rural Maine probably had numbers at least this high. Canneries in large population centers had bigger labor pools to draw from and would be less dependent on child workers. Most of these employees would be paid at a piece rate, thus productivity per hour was not a major consideration for the employers. The role of child labor was an issue that canning companies struggled with until after World War I. By then mechanization had displaced much of the hand work.[48] In addition to the large pool of unskilled and semi-skilled laborers, some highly skilled individuals like cappers, were needed when the canning season rolled around.

Year round employment was possible for tin-smiths who made cans by hand and box-makers who constructed wooden crates for shipping the canned goods. Labelers and shipping room helpers were also on call during the off-season to respond to purchase orders as they came in.

Corn shop size varied and smaller operations contracted with only a half dozen or so farmers and employed less than ten workers. Large canneries were supplied by over a hundred farms and needed hundreds of people to can the corn. A number of the companies also processed other foodstuffs (apples, blueberries, beans, squash, fish, etc.), thus extending both the list of products and the packing season.

In forty years, 1840-1879, the sweet corn canning industry had developed from the early experiments of Isaac Winslow into a considerable business stretching from Maine and Maryland to the Midwest. Evidence indicates that Maryland is second only to Maine in establishing the earliest corn canning plants. About 1865 Thomas Duckwell began canning corn in Clermont County, Ohio. Gilbert Van

Camp started processing corn at his Indianapolis, Indiana plant in 1861 and in 1868 the first canned Illinois sweet corn was processed by the Elgin Packing Company.[49]

Year	Percent of Labor Force Under Sixteen Years of Age
1879	18
1889	11
1899	9
1904	7
1909*	7
1914	5
1919*	3

Table 3.4   Children in U.S. Fruit and Vegetable Canning. *Includes fish packing. *Source*: *United States Census of Manufacturers,* various years.

The general geographic pattern of Maine corn canneries was beginning to develop by 1879 with a concentration in Cumberland County. Other factories were in Oxford, Franklin, Androscoggin, and Somerset Counties. Data for New Hampshire and Vermont are not available for this period. Three companies dominated Maine's sweet corn industry; J. Winslow Jones, Burnham & Morrill and Portland Packing, with the first being the most powerful. Fortunes were made by the owners. James P. Baxter's profits from Portland Packing Company laid the foundation of the family's wealth that would finance the political career of his son, Percival Baxter.[50] The younger Baxter was to become one of Maine's most popular governors, a philanthropist who donated the wilderness, Baxter State Park, home of the the state's highest peak, Mount Katahdin, to the people.

Chapter 4

Growth and Development of the Industry, 1880 - 1930

The Northern New England sweet corn industry experienced rapid growth during the half-century between 1880 and 1930. Maine had established a reputation for high quality canned corn and was earning awards at both national and international exhibits. Burnham & Morrill's Paris Sugar Corn trademark (1878) was to be a mainstay for the company until the 1960's when it ceased packing corn (Figure 4.1). Plants processing sweet corn increased from twenty-four to over one hundred (Table 4.1). Acreage, percent of all farms growing sweet corn and corn pack also expanded at about the same rate. Great advances were made in technical innovations concerned with improving canning processes, strains of sweet corn and agricultural methods. The composition of the corn shop labor force changed as children were largely phased out. This era also witnessed increased competition from other sweet corn producing areas.

Diffusion of Sweet Corn Canning Within Northern New England

By 1880 farmers in Maine were well aware of the benefits that could be gained growing sweet corn for canneries. During the 1870's there had been a gradual shift from general farming to dairying in Maine, New Hampshire and Vermont. This transition may be attributed in part to the influx of western beef to the eastern markets and the increased demand for dairy products in urban New England and New York. Sweet corn production offered these early dairymen a chance to

Figure 4.1   Award Winning Canned Corn. *Source*: B & M Division of B & G.

spread their economic risk. Day points out that much of the field corn acreage was replaced by sweet corn because of the development of the silo.

> Silos in Maine in 1880 could be counted on the fingers. Sixty years later they were standard equipment on the leading dairy farms and dairymen were using their corn to fill them. Another reason for the decline of corn as a grain crop was the growth of the sweet corn industry. In this case, sweet corn became a sharp contender with "yellow" corn for both land and labor. Also the dairy and sweet corn enterprises were closely related. Dairymen liked to grow sweet corn because it gave them a cash income and also it gave fodder and silage for their cattle.[1]

In addition to the cash income and cattle feed, some technologists believed the small family farms were well suited for the early sweet corn canning years. Family labor tended the small fields. At harvest time the same field was often picked twice. This usually resulted in higher quality since the late maturing ears were skipped during the first

Year	Maine	New Hampshire	Vermont	Total	Percent Reporting Only Corn*
1873	13	0	0	13	23.1
1880	24	0	0	24	47.8
1890	93	0	0	93	19.0
1900	95	1	4	100	27.1
1910	94	1	9	104	22.6
1920	111	2	10	123	24.8
1930	97	3	9	109	24.8
1940	75	2	5	82	24.7
1950	58	1	4	63	14.3
1960	15	1	3	19	5.3
1968	1	0	0	1	0

Table 4.1   Vegetable Canneries. *Source:* Compiled by author; see sources for Figure 1.2; *Percent Reporting Only Corn, data from state registers.

picking. Also manure, which was plentiful on dairy farms and stockpiled during the winter months, was widely used as a fertilizer to which sweet corn responded fairly well.[2] John Donald Black in his classic work, *The Rural Economy of New England*, considers the farm-sweet corn relationship to be the following:

The farm economy factors in the situation (sweet corn production) are as follows: First, the farms of the far north territory need a cultivated crop for their rotation systems. The season is too short for field corn. The other choice, potatoes, calls for a good bit of equipment which can be used economically only on larger acreages than most of these farmers wish to till... Second, sweet corn really needs manure as a fertilizer. Commercial fertilizer will serve only as a supplement to it. The dairy farmers of New England customarily put their manure first of all on the tilled crops which they plant. Manure is not a good fertilizer for potatoes. Third, the green sweet corn stalks and husks make a very good supplement to the pastures which are at their poorest in the late summer. Most good dairy farmers grow some succulent forage for their cows at this period. Fourth, the labor in sweet corn conflicts very little with the haying and other farm work. The children can help with hoeing and harvesting during the summer vacation. Fifth, no special equipment is required. The canning factories furnish the seed and more or less supervision.[3]

From the late 1800's to 1929, the percentage of all farms producing sweet corn grew from about five to thirteen percent. In Maine it reached eighteen percent and in the most conducive areas, such as Oxford County, nearly a third of the farmers were growing the crop (Figure 4.2). Of the twenty-four corn canning plants operating in Maine by 1880, thirteen were in Cumberland County, close to Portland, where the industry started. A second significant cluster of corn shops had developed in the Sandy River Valley of southern Franklin County around Farmington and Wilton (Figure 3.4b). Forty-eight percent of all shops processed only sweet corn. The remainder canned sweet corn and other vegetables, fruits or fish.

In 1881 this budding industry experienced an unsettling event. John Winslow Jones and his company met with economic failure. This was big news for *The Maine Farmer*. The January 12, 1882 edition states that one of Jones' major problems was over-expansion. With British backing he had constructed eight new canning factories and retained little for working capital. At the time of his failure Jones' liabilities amounted to $340,000 and was considered to be the largest bankruptcy in Maine up to 1881.[4] In 1882 the remains of Jones' canning empire were reorganized into the Winslow Packing Company. Although farmers' faith had been shaken, Winslow Packing Company did a considerable amount of business processing sweet corn and lobsters. In 1887 this company sold 203,000 cases of canned corn at $1.10 to $1.25 per dozen cans. Portland Packing Company later took control of Winslow Packing Company and purchased its brand names.

Shortly after Jones' failure, another wave of unrest swept across the sweet corn industry in Northern New England. Price control for raw sweet corn was entirely under the direction of the canners. This policy led the sweet corn growing farmers of Maine to negotiate for an increase in the price of the raw product. In March 1882 a large number of sweet corn producers from Cumberland, York, Oxford, Franklin and Somerset Counties met with the corn packers at Portland. After

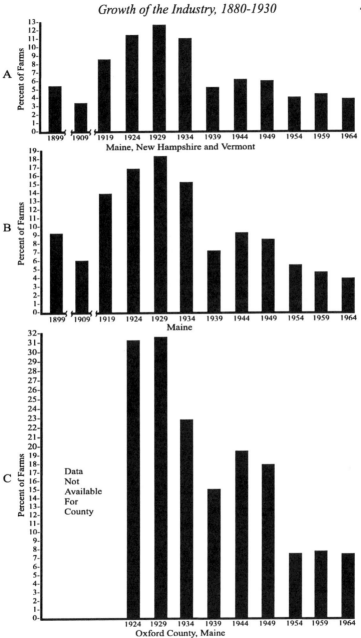

Figure 4.2   Percent of All Farms Growing Sweet Corn. *Source:* Computed by author from U.S. Census of Agriculture; data for 1909 include only farms reporting 1 or more acres of sweet corn. Data for 1904 and 1914 not available by state.

extensive discussion between committees representing each side, no agreement could be reached. Once this attempt at collective bargaining failed, the growers recommended by a vote of fifty-six to zero that sweet corn should not be grown for less than two and one-half cents per pound cut from the cob.[5] In June *The Maine Farmer* reported that farmers planted about 12,500 acres of sweet corn to be processed in seventy-one different factories scattered throughout the state. The number of shops had nearly tripled in two years and there was an increase in acreage over the preceding years. The three leading corn canning companies, which controlled about half the factories, paid the following prices that year: Portland Packing, two cents a pound; Burnham & Morrill, three and a half cents for a twenty-six-ounce can; and Winslow Packing, three and a half cents for a twenty-six-ounce can.[6] The practice of purchasing raw corn by the pound, which Portland Packing began in 1882, was later adopted by other companies.

Following these two rather exciting years in Maine corn canning, the business settled into a period of rapid and constant growth. The number of corn canning plants increased from twenty-four to ninety-three in the ten years between 1880 and 1890. Although the greatest factory density remained in Cumberland County, noticeable increases were made in Oxford, Franklin, Somerset, Kennebec, Androscoggin and York counties. Establishments also appeared in Penobscot, Waldo, Knox, Lincoln, and Sagadahoc Counties during this time (Figure 3.4c).

When a company decided to construct a cannery in a town, it meant that farmers would have an added source of income and the local people would be able to earn money as seasonally employed corn shop workers. These early plants varied greatly in size and number of employees. Thirty or forty acres might be a season's supply for a small operation run by a dozen or so people; whereas, a large cannery with one hundred seasonal workers would require hundreds of acres of sweet corn to support it. The physical size of the factories also differed greatly from a small shed of a few hundred square feet to large buildings enclosing great amounts of space not only for processing, but also for storage of the canned product. One of the large Maine canneries of the 1880's was constructed at Unity, Waldo County, in 1887.

In May, 1887 the Portland Packing Company began building its twenty-eighth cannery at Unity. A local newspaper correspondent reported, "The buildings of the corn packing factory are now underway and are larger than originally stated. The main building is to be two hundred and forty feet. The husking house will be eighty by twenty feet and the engine house thirty by twenty feet".[7]

The decade of the 90's saw the number of corn factories increase to one hundred. The geographical distribution spread to include Piscataquis County, Maine; Carroll County, New Hampshire; and Windsor County, Vermont (Figure 3.4d). The Windsor plant is of special interest because of its size. "In 1896 a corn canning factory was built. It was then the largest of its kind in New England, having a capacity of 1,200,000 cans annually."[8] By 1899, Samuel T. Pickard in his history of Portland, considers the corn canning industry a major contributor to the economy of not only the city, but the entire state.

> The development of the canning business has...been an important feature of the industrial prosperity of Maine, owing partly to the fact that the climate and soil of this state produce a quality of corn that cannot be matched in other states, and also to the fact that the system of canning now in use was a Portland invention. All over the interior of Maine may be found corn factories owned by Portland merchants...[9]

Although this statement probably over-emphasizes the role of the climate and soil, it does give an indication of the extent of the region's corn canning in the late 1890's.

One hundred and four plants processed corn in 1910. Five new factories appeared in Vermont (Figure 3.4e). The establishments at Brattleboro, Essex, Windsor and Westminster were owned by a Maine company, H. C. Baxter and Brothers. Vermont concerns ran four other corn canneries. Changes were under way in the older sweet corn areas of Maine. The rise of the Monmouth Canning Company under the direction of Elwin A. Soule is one of the more important. The company was founded in 1905 when Soule acquired a plant in Monmouth from a local committee that had built it. Earlier, Soule had directed a shop at Gorham and, at one time, attempted to operate a factory in Gardiner. In 1909 Monmouth Company expanded, adding a plant at Union. That same year Seth H. Soule entered the company and took an active part in the family business.[10]

This expansion in numbers of corn canneries continued until after the First World War (Figure 3.4f). New companies were formed and old ones expanded, frequently changing owners. The Black and Gay Company originated at this time. According to T. L. S. Morse, "On November 16, 1911, Fred C. Black and George Gay acquired the J. O. Cushing Company canning factory at Thomaston."[11] Although this business never became large, it is an example of a firm that played a significant role in the local area around Knox and Lincoln Counties. One of the well documented accounts of establishing a canning plant concerns the one at Starks, Maine. An item appears among the unpublished notes of Nellie Frederic, a resident of Starks, somewhat of a local historian and my grandmother. According to her chronicle:

> Back in 1914 or 1915 the rumor somehow got around that ...Frank Noyes who owned a corn factory over in Carmel...was desirous of moving or selling it. It was located in the midst of potato land, where there was too much clay for successful corn raising, making the operation of a corn factory anything but a paying proposition. Two enterprising Starks citizens...heard about it and realized its possibilities. They went out into the country talking it over with the farmers, and ...finally consulted with the owner of the Carmel shop. He made the following proposition:
>
> If they would raise by subscription $1,000 among the Starks people, the would-be planters and anyone else interested in the project or get them to sign up for its equivalent in either work or money to enable him to tear down and move the shop, and to rebuild it; if they would contract for 300 acres of corn to be canned fall (1916); further, if they could get the selectmen to agree to exempt him from taxation for five years, he would be willing to try his luck in Starks. Once again ..., they traveled through the country with horse and sleigh, interviewing the farmers... they were able to meet all the requirements in time to move the factory and have it ready to operate when the corn was ripe. However, because the farmers were not experienced in raising sweet corn, and because so much of the land that spring was too wet to work early enough for corn, when canning time came, harvest from only 150 acres, about half what they contracted for, was hauled to the shop. Some of it wasn't planted at all, some of it failed to grow in the wet soil, and the frost came before other fields had time to mature, but they were all learning about the raising and canning of sweet corn and were not displeased with their progress.[12]

This account indicates the extent to which many of the small communities desired a corn shop. The newspaper from a nearby town carried the following announcement of its opening.

An event of considerable importance from a commercial and agricultural standpoint was the starting of the F. F. Noyes Corn Shop Thursday afternoon. The shop, which was one of several run by Mr. Noyes, was moved to Starks from Carmel. It is located near what is said by experts to be some of the finest corn land in the state. It is estimated that the land in this vicinity will yield 2,500 cans to the acre, which is a high average. It is expected that the pack this year will amount to about a quarter of a million cans. The shop is...equipped with six husking machines, and one of the new automatic sealing machines in which no solder is used. The shop is lighted by electricity furnished by its own dynamo, and the motive power is furnished by a steam plant. Owing to the improved machinery a crew of 25 persons will be required to operate the plant.[13]

Noyes operated this plant for one year and sold it to the Monmouth Canning Company in 1917.[14]

By 1920 one hundred and twenty-three factories were processing sweet corn in Maine, New Hampshire and Vermont. A quarter of these were concerned only with corn. This, following the World War One economic boom, was the high point in number of corn shops.

During this expansion both the canners and growers attempted to become better organized. The canning interest within Maine formed a group known as the Maine Canners Association. A letter from John W. Gault to F. Webster Browne discloses:

The Maine Canners Association was organized April 29, 1912. ...There were 19 Charter Members...The high mark for membership was in the early 1920's. Our 50 members operating 127 factories...nearly 100 were corn factories packing about 2,500,000 cases of mostly Crosby or white corn.[15]

Later the constitution of this association was amended to allow membership to companies in New Hampshire, Vermont and Massachusetts. The Maine Canners Association did not include all of the corn processors in Northern New England, but the larger concerns and many of the small companies took an active role in the organization.

A few years after the formation of the Canners Association, sweet corn growers made an effort to consolidate. In 1919 the Maine Sweet Corn Growers Association came into being. Maine's Commissioner of Agriculture report indicated three major objectives of the growers association: to encourage farmers to use more efficient methods of culture and thus obtain greater yields and reduce the cost of production, to represent growers in their contracts with canners, and to cooperate with the canners for the betterment of the industry.[16]

At first, these two organizations cooperated fairly well with each other, but as happened in the 1880's, dissention developed. Day points out that such things as uniform grower contracts, use of locally grown seed, and quick payment for corn by canners were among problems resolved by the two groups. In 1918, because of the war boom, cut sweet corn was bringing a high price of five cents per pound. For 1919 the canners planned to pay only four cents but this was quickly increased to a nickel a pound. It is possible that growers considered this a minor victory. Prices for 1920 were acceptable to both sides and times were good for grower and canner, but the post-World War One recession had begun and in 1921 trouble developed.

> ...the canners announced that they could pay only three cents a pound... The packers refused to negotiate...The farmers cut their plantings sharply and some factories did not operate at all. The next year the growers were unable to even get a meeting with the canners.[17]

There was considerable disagreement over the exact causes that forced the two associations apart. Since the Growers Association dissolved during the 1920's there are few records to indicate the general attitude toward the canners or the various state agencies. On the other hand, the minutes of the Maine Canners Association are available. Business discussions among the canners demonstrate the changing position of the sweet corn processors. At the December 17, 1919 meeting a paper was read that illustrated, from accounts of ninety-one sweet corn growers, the net cost to farmers per acre of sweet corn was $101.63.[18] This interest in raw corn production cost indicates relatively close relations with the farmers. Although details are not recorded at the June 28, 1921 meeting, the canners voted to accept a new style of growers' contract.[19] Again, close cooperation is demonstrated. By March 1922 this canner-grower relationship had changed greatly, as noted by the fact that the canners voted to take no action in relation to the request by F. O. Washburn, Commissioner of Agriculture of the State of Maine, for a meeting between the Maine Canners Association, Sweet Corn Growers Association, Department of Agriculture, and the Extension Service of the College of Agriculture.[20]

With the failure of the growers' association, all collective bargaining between the farmers and the canners disappeared, while the corn canners reverted to a take-it or leave-it policy as far as prices were concerned. In Day's *Farming in Maine 1860-1940* it is pointed out that, "One result of all this agitation and acrimony was the establishment of two farmer-owned canning plants, one at Dexter and the other at Farmington."[21] Once tempers had subsided and the necessity of cooperating became apparent, interaction between the two factors began to improve. In his 1924, report the Commissioner of Agriculture noted that, "Relations between growers and canners, somewhat strained for several years, have become more cordial with the establishment of a higher scale of prices. Reports for 1924 indicate a return to normal...."[22] During the remainder of the 20's dealings between farmers and processors continued on a reasonably friendly basis.

Although several new corn canning plants were constructed during the decade between 1920 and 1930, the total number of establishments decreased from one hundred and twenty-three to one hundred and nine (Figure 3.4.g and Table 4.1). In some cases factories were moved to new locations. According to Adrian Wells Sr., owner of the W. S. Wells Canning Company at Wilton, Maine, his grandfather, Walter S. Wells, founded the business in Anson in 1894 and moved it to Wilton in 1912.[23] Other communities built and operated canneries before selling them to private companies. The agricultural interests and businessmen of Freedom felt that the construction of such a plant would be to their advantage. In 1922 Freedom and nearby towns formed a group to bring a canning plant to the area. The Freedom Canning Company, as the investors were called, sold shares at $10.00 to get money to build. In 1923 this new enterprise canned corn and the Monmouth Canning Company purchased the plant the following winter.[24] Liberty soon followed in the footsteps of Freedom and a local committee built a factory which was quickly rented to Soule and his Monmouth Canning Company. Community pride seems to bubble in the photo that today graces one of the town's historic postcards (Figure 4.3). It's hard to determine if its the work crew or a Sunday church outing!

Corn shops often doubled as halls for public events. Records of the McIntire-Sawin camp, a summer facility on Papoose Pond in the Waterford, Maine, area, include an August 15, 1912, entry that "Kathleen and Glenn went home to go to the dance at the corn shop. They remember a big party at the warehouse but are vague about

Figure 4.3   Corn Canning Factory, Liberty, Maine, 1920's. *Source:* Liberty
Graphics.

details."[25] This is a fairly typical teenage response, 1912 or 2001! The
warehouse would have been empty of canned goods in mid-August and
a wonderful place for dancing. New canneries were also constructed at
Mercer, Maine; Shelburne, Vermont; and Pittsfield and Hampstead, New
Hampshire.

Pack statistics first appear in 1889 when 505,362 cases of twenty-
four number two cans of corn were processed in Maine. By 1910 sweet
corn production reached 1,487,000 cases and continued to increase
through World War One (Figure 4.4 and Table 4.2). Vermont and
New Hampshire pack data are not available before 1930. By 1920
sweet corn production had increased to 1,588,000 cases. This rise in
canned corn production continued into the 20's and by 1930 well over
1,900,000 cases were run through the region's corn shops. Although the
number of factories decreased, output increased during the 20's.

Acreage is another indication of corn canning diffusion within
Northern New England. The United States Census of Agriculture first
lists sweet corn acreage as a separate item in 1899. Acreage increased

Figure 4.4   Part of 1910 Pack, Thomas and Marble Corn Shop, Wilton, Maine. According to Mary Croswell, provider of the photo, the woman on the left is her Aunt Edith Stanley, who was 15 years old at the time. *Source*: Mary Croswell.

significantly between that year and 1929 (Figure 4.5). In 1909 sweet corn covered 10,392 acres with 84 percent of it in Maine. It is reasonable to assume that most of this crop went into cans, although undoubtedly a small portion found its way to the fresh market. The greatest concentration of acreage was in areas with the largest number of canneries. By 1919 Oxford, Somerset, Kennebec, Cumberland, Androscoggin and Franklin Counties in Maine all grew over 1,000 acres of various varieties of sweet corn, and over 13,000 acres were planted to sweet corn in the three northern New England states. The geographical distribution of this production remained constant through the 1920's with Oxford County leading in total acreage. The greatest producing county outside of Maine was Chittenden in Vermont, which had two canneries operating in 1930 (Table 4.3).

Year	State or States	Pack
1889	Maine	= 505,362[a]
1899	Maine	= 710,419[a]
1910	Maine	= 1,487,000[a]
1920	Maine	= 1,588,000[a]
1930	Maine and Vermont	= 1,929,864[a]
1940	Maine, New Hampshire and Vermont	= 794,123[a]
1950	Maine, New Hampshire and Vermont	= 526,390[a]
1960	Maine, New Hampshire and Vermont	= 603,000[b]

[a] Cases of twenty-four #2 cans

[b] Cases of twenty-four #303 cans

Table 4.2   Sweet Corn Pack in Northern New England, 1889 - 1960. *Source:* Compiled by Norman Elliott from statistics of the National Canners Association, Unpublished Notes, 1967.

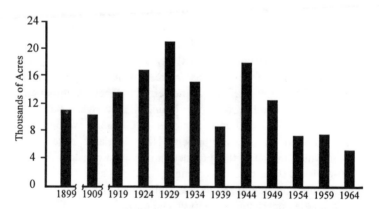

Figure 4.5   Maine, New Hampshire and Vermont, Sweet Corn Acreage. Data not available for 1904 and 1914. Value for 1899 includes Maine only. Data for 1909 includes only farms reporting 1 or more acres of sweet corn. *Source:* United States Census of Agriculture.

County	1919	1924	1929	1934	1939	1944	1949	1954	1959	1964
Androscoggin	1,150	1,426	1,519	1,274	637	2,075	788	316	295	142
Aroostook	2	1	4	31	11	3	21	9	11	9
Cumberland	1,390	1,424	1,237	1,055	415	1,073	547	358	330	430
Franklin	1,058	1,042	1,416	1,026	516	1,475	958	302	319	157
Hancock	27	55	35	31	71	206	25	10	10	26
Kennebec	1,398	1,618	2,094	1,308	574	1,805	1,103	265	318	230
Knox	147	168	319	252	119	116	62	30	17	160
Lincoln	170	216	126	79	24	29	54	26	155	46
Oxford	2,604	2,025	3,702	2,170	1,591	2,522	1,840	942	1,314	535
Penobscot	650	1,005	1,163	603	554	1,000	827	509	590	254
Piscataquis	157	136	16	44	102	51	169	244	41	27
Sagadahoc	52	55	91	63	89	165	98	35	184	87
Somerset	1,595	1,927	2,738	1,680	662	2,215	2,030	802	809	42
Waldo	360	707	1,137	915	437	1,208	1,047	424	342	107
Washington	10	4	27	10	11	7	15	12	11	11
York	546	947	819	694	400	571	223	201	168	180
Total	11,316	12,574	16,443	11,235	6,268	14,512	9,807	4,485	4,914	2,443

Table 4.3a   Sweet Corn Acreage by Counties, Maine 1919 - 1964.

County	1919	1924	1929	1934	1939	1944	1949	1954	1959	1964
Belknap	24	206	147	152	67	128	70	70	193	42
Carroll	225	336	306	321	137	426	288	149	90	85
Cheshire	70	81	120	82	58	43	46	57	60	41
Coos	7	7	5	9	3	8	32	104	56	17
Grafton	83	70	145	80	63	50	56	79	39	63
Hillsborough	237	456	428	552	315	574	522	538	727	712
Merrimack	70	303	400	456	188	322	287	320	302	146
Rockingham	412	472	548	545	292	388	380	391	337	294
Stafford	71	129	179	139	68	103	65	116	65	79
Sullivan	48	122	99	38	34	26	48	30	26	27
Total	1,247	2,182	2,377	2,374	1,225	2,068	1,794	1,854	1,895	1,506

Table 4.3b   Sweet Corn Acreage by Counties, New Hampshire 1919 - 1964.

County	1919	1924	1929	1934	1939	1944	1949	1954	1959	1964
Addison	8	16	15	31	25	15	20	24	24	17
Bennington	13	45	66	70	37	86	26	42	29	12
Caledonia	24	18	38	32	22	16	18	15	14	25
Chittenden	330	466	646	647	403	534	347	372	330	201
Essex	-	1	12	4	7	1	5	3	-	1
Franklin	50	267	169	144	106	13	44	28	60	51
Grand Isle	191	207	182	8	5	14	7	8	5	17
Lamoille	1	2	15	14	13	74	78	98	11	30
Orange	147	197	256	155	187	207	223	154	15	23
Orleans	4	16	40	19	1 7	10	15	24	22	16
Rutland	24	56	77	63	31	41	35	48	59	96
Washington	42	168	198	193	130	153	128	70	47	41
Windham	208	319	306	59	88	77	58	88	70	117
Windsor	81	281	178	68	72	60	34	48	55	62
Total	1,123	2,039	2,198	1,507	1,143	1,301	1,038	1,021	741	709

Table 4.3c   Sweet Corn Acreage by County, Vermont, 1919 - 1964.

Grand Total	13,686	16,795	21,018	15,116	8,636	17,881	12,639	7,317	7,550	4,658

Table 4.3   Sweet Corn Acreage. *Source:* Census of Agriculture.

Innovations Within the Industry

Many technical innovations in canning methods, plant breeding and agricultural practices influenced the sweet corn processing business between 1880 and 1930.

Canning Innovations

The half-century between 1880 and 1930 witnessed a continual parade of new machinery and techniques linked to canning corn and other foods. Old methods were improved and new ones developed. The first truly efficient continuous corn cooker appeared in 1884 as a result of experiments carried out by John C. Winters of Mount Morris, New York.[26] This invention was soon followed by a revised version of the corn cutter which replaced the one perfected by Barker. Welcome Sprague developed this new cutter and had it on the market by 1888. Sprague's manufacturing headquarters were moved to Hoopeston, Illinois, from New York; this business later played an important role in the production of many types of canning equipment.[27] William H. Sells, a self-employed inventor from Green Bay, Wisconsin, created a practical corn husker in 1890; by 1900 its use was widespread in corn factories throughout the United States.[28] Another important step in the reduction of hand labor came in 1894 when the first patent on a can closing machine (capper) was issued to J. A. Steward of Rutland, Vermont.[29] In 1898 Frank W. Smith of Portland, Maine, received a patent for an agitating cooker that gave corn and other vegetables an excellent cooking while in the can.[30] In 1903 two significant patents were issued to men in Greenwood, Indiana. John Jennings had perfected an improved method of steam cooking the contents of unclosed cans and Ralph B. Polk developed a series of belts and carriers to increase the speed with which canned goods could be handled within the canning factory.[31] Inventions similar to these were numerous around the turn of the century. A few years later, Henry Forhan, a Portland, Maine, corn canner, built an apparatus to increase the efficiency of cooking canned goods by revolving and shaking the full cans as they were heated.[32]

Beginning about 1905 corn black, which had been a minor problem during the late 1800's, started to appear in canned corn at an increasing rate. After the industry began using machine made cans rather than hand-made and hand-coated ones, it suddenly became of great concern.

Extensive experimentation found that a chemical reaction between gases given off by the cooking corn and the iron in the tin cans formed black spots in the corn. A coating of zinc oxide enamel over the tin plating would prevent corn black from developing in machine-produced cans.[33] George Jewett, who gained his early experience with J. Winslow Jones and Burnham & Morrill, developed (1903) a self-heating can to increase convenience for the consumer. He later (1910) founded his own canning company in Norridgewock, Maine.[34] By 1908, adopted innovations connected with corn canning (the husker, the cutter, the hot pack process and the sanitary can) were so extensive that the corn industry was well positioned for the new century. Other than perfection of vacuum packing foods without including liquids, most of the improvements in corn canning machinery and techniques between 1910 and 1930 focused on modifying existing processes. Fred F. Fitzgerald of the American Can Company developed the vacuum pack in 1926. The first company to pack corn by this method, Minnesota Valley Canning Company (later the Green Giant Company) of Le Suer, Minnesota, put up 1,896 cases of 10.5 ounce cans in the fall of 1928.[35]

Plant Breeding Innovations

Tremendous effort went into the improvement of sweet corn varieties. Some of this experimentation was undertaken in Northern New England but the greatest concentration was in the Midwest. These fifty years (1880-1930) include three rather distinct periods of different types of sweet corn. Huelsen, in his *Sweet Corn*, divides the usage of different varieties into eras which depend upon the popularity of the various types. Often changes in consumer habits were not immediately felt by processors, but eventually they had to conform to the demands of the public.

Up to 1890, earliness, usually associated with dwarfness of plant, was the major factor in the success of a variety and practically all varieties had white kernels. Only a few types with large ears were known at that time. Breeding was mainly concerned with selection of large eared, early maturing types. In 1902 Burpee introduced Golden Bantam, the first popular yellow variety, the high quality of which dissociated yellow corn as an indicator of poor quality. The third phase, consisting of inbreeding followed by crossing, came into its own in 1918, when breeders employed by public agencies started work on a systematic basis.[36]

As with the early white sweet corn types, the first commercial yellow sweet corn evolved from the efforts of a few private individuals who were experimenting with plant reproduction and improvement. Golden Bantam was developed from stock owned by William Chambers of Greenfield, Massachusetts, who began work on a yellow sweet corn before 1885. After his death, W. Atlee Burpee Company of Philadelphia acquired some of his seed.[37] Golden Bantam improved in quality and increased in quantity of production until it challenged and then replaced white sweet corn as the leading canned corn.

Once Golden Bantam had reached the market and consumer response had been noted, increased effort was put into sweet corn breeding programs throughout the corn canning regions. A factor that contributed to the rise of Golden Bantam was its ability to resist bacterial wilt. Bacterial wilt or Stewart's Disease caused widespread sweet corn damage during the early years of the twentieth century. In 1929 a serious outbreak of the disease occurred. Glenn M. Smith of Purdue University had worked extensively with this problem during the 1920's and by 1930 he had perfected a Golden Bantam plant that resisted Stewart's Disease.[38]

Following the First World War, increased research went into developing a variety of yellow sweet corn that could respond well to the physical conditions of Maine, New Hampshire and Vermont. Several strains of Golden Bantam were perfected at the University of Maine Experiment Station, but in general, these early yellow sweet corn varieties that were grown in Northern New England did not perform so well as those developed in the Midwest. During the 1920's most of the corn canners in the three states considered the locally grown seed corn the best for canning, because it was supposedly adapted to the micro-environments. Miles E. Langley, an official of the Portland Packing Company, presented this policy in a letter dated November 22, 1924:

> ...I am convinced that the only seed policy which the Maine packer should follow is to go in the spring to the best farmer you have, having the best corn ground, give him the best seed available, have him understand that the acreage subscribed is to be used for seed, watch it carefully during the season to see that every detail of growing is properly attended to, make a personal survey of the piece at the time it is in suitable canning condition, tag them from the healthiest plants in the healthiest sections of the piece, ears which conform to your idea of Fancy Crosby Corn, avoiding eccentricities such as twin ears, very early or very late

maturity, very large or very small row number, or very long or very short ears. Tag twice as many ears as you expect to need for seed and make a further selection in the dry house when this seed is ready to shell. I am convinced that if this policy is followed for a few years the canner will see a material improvement in the uniformity of his crop and the yield in pounds per acre.[39]

With attitudes such as Langley's, Northern New England canners continued to process large amounts of the white Crosby corn as well as an increased amount of Golden Bantam during the second decade of the twentieth century. By 1930 United States sweet corn canners had settled on four principal open pollinated varieties of corn. Huelsen evaluates each of these as follows:

1. Evergreen strains: This type has a tough hull (pericarp), matures rather slowly, and has the ability to withstand both a wide range of conditions and considerable abuse from the grower. The seed is easy to grow and has always been the cheapest on the market. Although the cob is usually large, the cut corn percentage is good. Evergreen has always been and still is to some extent the standby of the small canner who finds difficulty in setting up efficient quality control.

Early Evergreen and Narrow Grain Evergreen are the only two strains of interest to the canners.

Early Evergreen matures about a week earlier than Stowell's Evergreen. It could be used to extend the canning season and also grown in the north where it reaches canning stage at about the same time as Crosby.

Narrow Grained Evergreen seems to be higher in quality than Stowell's Evergreen.

2. Country Gentlemen: Long the quality variety of the Corn Belt and Tri-State area (Maryland, Delaware and Virginia). It matures much faster than Evergreen and is generally confined to packers of high quality corn. It requires fertile soils, high organic matter and its climatic range is restricted to the southern areas of the corn canning areas.

3. Crosby: Made Maine sweet corn famous. The variety is reasonably early, producing fairly large ears with 12-16 rows. It is primarily an early type.

4.   Golden Bantam: First yellow variety to achieve popularity.   Good quality and high sugar content.   Has a flavor quite different from other types, possibly due to its flint origin.[40]

Agricultural Innovations

The many agricultural ideas introduced between 1880 and 1930 brought a revolution to farms of America. During the late 1800's, horse-drawn equipment was greatly improved and by the turn of the century such items as mowing machines, horse rakes, manure spreaders, seed-sowers, and small-grain harvesters were in widespread use. Silos reflect change in livestock feeds and storage methods. With improved design, preservation of corn fodder (including sweet corn waste) made for greater and steadier milk production (Figure 4.6).[41] During the first thirty years of the twentieth century, the multi-purpose farm tractor inspired mechanical innovations by farmers. Expanding farm mechanization meant a reduction in the agricultural labor force and a greater production capacity per individual farmer. The sweet corn grower, who was usually a general farmer, was as quick as any other agriculturalist to adopt the tractor and other recent inventions.

In addition to new equipment that was directly connected with tilling the soil and harvesting the crop, the motor truck played a significant role in agriculture. It gave farmers the ability to move their products from field or barn to processors or fresh market in a fairly short time. Both the sweet corn canners and growers found this to their advantage. The quicker sweet corn can be transported from the field to the can the higher will be its sugar content. As the truck replaced the horse drawn cart, time between picking and canning was greatly reduced. Trucks could also haul larger loads than horses. This development resulted in increased size of corn canneries because corn could be transported greater distances with trucks than by draft animals. Canneries were able to service larger areas with more farmers and greater acreage. An example of increasing service area appears in Nellie Frederic's notes.

> In those days (1920's) when corn was hauled to the factory with teams, there was an average of forty-five loads brought every day...On such days there were often six or seven teams in line waiting for their turns on the scales. Nowdays (1940)... there is an average of thirty to thirty-five truck loads. When corn was hauled with horses, a large percentage of the acreage was contracted in Starks, but since trucks came

Figure 4.6   Silo. This layout in the Frederic barn, Starks, Maine, is representative of early interior silos New England farmers would construct in a barn bay. The octagonal design approaches a circular shape, which is most efficient in preventing fodder spoiling air pockets from forming during filling. Many farmers didn't have the resources or skill to construct a round silo. The octagonal could be built with simple materials and modest carpentry abilities. A plaster coating on its interior wall helped make it airtight. On a cold, snow blown day in winter, the dairyman was happy to have feed in the barn close to the cows. *Source:* Author.

into common use, farmers in... surrounding towns have planted corn for the Starks factory.[42]

The advent of trucks resulted in sweet corn being grown as much as twenty or thirty miles from a cannery and still being processed soon enough to be of acceptable quality. Traditional spatial relationships between growers and canneries changed as transport technology improved.[43]

New agricultural techniques appeared along with innovations in equipment. Much attention was devoted to crop rotation and soil conservation practices. Increasing damage caused by the European corn borer during the early years of the twentieth century created great alarm among both growers and processors. Each state with a significant sweet corn industry began supporting research to combat the pest. In a study conducted by the University of New Hampshire, the following conclusion was reached:

> In... the records of three consecutive years it is found that about 60 percent of the borers exhibit two generations under New Hampshire conditions... only a small percentage of the second generation of larvae are able to over-winter successfullly. Such of these larvae as do survive the winter and pupate successfully the next spring, develop into adults of small size, which appear to be capable of producing only a relatively small number of eggs. Apparently there is a limiting factor here in relation to normal increase of this species under field conditions in New Hampshire. It covers a wide territory, but the intensity of infection is light.[44]

In light of these and other findings made during the 1920's, agreement was reached that one of the most effective ways to control the corn borer was to deep plow old corn fields. At first many growers resisted changing their plowing and cultivating practices, but, as increased information spread throughout the countryside, deep plowing became more widely adopted, and the European corn borer hazard slowly receded.

Farmers

American farmers were enjoying prosperity during this fifty-year-run

(1880-1930). Innovations were making life easier on the farm (in the field, barn and home). Transportation and food preservation technology linked rural places to urban markets. The boom in demand for farm goods during World War One was followed by a slower but still healthy economy of the Roaring Twenties. Maine, New Hampshire and Vermont rode this wave of growth in commercial farming. Many rural families were not part of the transformation and remained stuck in the lifestyle and conditions of mid-19th century subsistence agriculture. This dicotomy was especially pronounced in much of Northern New England.[45]

As canning factories spread, sweet corn became ingrained in the lives of many farmers. Leroy Sanderson and his son Burton grew sweet corn for local canneries in Waterford and Harrison on their farm in East Waterford, Maine. Burton (age 12 in 1890) kept a diary.

1890, June 3, "Planted a little corn"
1890, September 16, "Addison Millett (field-man for local corn shop) was here to look at sweet corn."
1890, September 17, "Hauled load of sweet corn to North Waterford."
1891, September 7, "Addison Millett said corn would be ready next week."
1891, September 13, "Mr. Abraham Norwood (a neighbor) helped get corn to North Waterford"
1900, August 22, "I visited E. (Ephraim) Jillson in Otisfield. Jillson was busy getting his corn shop ready to start canning."
1900, September 10, "Last of Sanderson corn was picked and sent to Harrison."[46]

Burton's visit was probably to see his friend, George, Ephraim's son. In 1912, George acquired the business, a success until his untimely death in 1924.[47] Farmers and canners were often friends; in some cases, individuals were involved with both ends of the enterprise.

The Frederic Farm in Starks expanded and commercialized between 1880 and 1930. The family arrived on what is now Chicken Street in 1795 and by 1880 had acquired about 150 acres of mixed farm and forest land. This included 20 acres of prime bottomland with Fryeburg soil. The operation was largely subsistence with modest amounts of hay, maple syrup, grain, milk, eggs, wool and timber being sold. My grandfather, Marcelles Frederic (born 1857) had taken over most management decisions by 1890; but, it continued as a semi-commercial operation and the family did well. He added draft horse raising to the farm business and expanded dairying. The possibility that a corn cannery might be attracted to Starks held his interest and he supported such an effort. With its construction in 1916, he planted his first sweet corn. He was happy to realize this dream and celebrated his May 25 birthday by planting some corn for the shop on that date each year until his death in 1942.

Despite this movement toward new ideas and markets, he never learned to drive an automobile, rejected tractors and was suspicious of horse drawn (ground-driven) manure spreaders. His son, Glenn (born 1903) had no such reservations. By 1930, lumber production (timber acreage had been added), milk, and sweet corn were the principal sources of family income. Electrical power had arrived at the farm in 1927, and beginning in 1929 public roads were plowed in winter. I still have grandfather Marcelles' sleigh that was purchased in 1928, the year before roads were plowed. Its been stored in the family barn since and has very low mileage!

The Frederic family adjusted to agricultural change. Other members of the farm community were reluctant to adapt. Among our neighbors, some took advantage of new opportunities in agriculture and made profits, whereas others fell by the wayside or left for jobs in milltowns. Farms with marginal land bases and limited working capital were most likely to fail and those that remained tended to expand in size. Rural Northern New England had undergone a revolution; the lights came on by a flick of a switch, the highway was open for cars and trucks year round and sweet corn was a good deal. The cloud of depression was gathering on the horizon, but the few that noticed thought it would be only a brief shower.

Labor

Sweet corn growing and processing provided seasonal employment for thousands of people in Maine, New Hampshire and Vermont. Field labor at harvest time included traditional farm hands, housewives and children, as well as others that wished to pick up a bit of money. One needed to know a ripe ear from one that wasn't and that was the only significant skill. The big trick was to have a picking crew when the corn was ready for canning. Some individuals in the farm community would move from grower to grower as needed. Canners and farmers worked out a planting timetable in the spring to ensure that the harvest was spread out over the entire canning season thus avoiding oversupply of corn on some days and a shortage on others. Weather conditions during the growing and picking seasons were risky and often reality and the plan would not be the same.

Cannery workers numbered about 7,500 in 1899 and received a total payroll of $349,000.[48] This averages about $46 per worker for the four to six week season. These workers came from the local community and often included handicapped and the young; "Husking gives employment to many inferior people and children who otherwise could not profitably be employed."[49] From 1880-1920, the percentage of fruit and vegetable cannery labor force made up of children was significant (Table 3.4). Children provided a flexible labor pool that early canners found attractive. Small children who came to work with their mothers posed a problem. The little ones would often play around their mothers at work because the concept of day care was not understood by most owners. As time passed, government regulations clashed with child labor. The passage of child labor laws, school attendance regulations, mechanization, and the general rise in family incomes reduced the number of underage workers in canneries.[50] Jillson's 1912 corn shop crew in Otisfield (Figure 4.7) indicates the high dependency on child labor. When in 1919 his company introduced the first husking machines into that area, demand for underage workers dropped. New technology contributed to loss of jobs and the closing of some of the smaller, under- capitalized operations such as the nearby Stone's canning factory which became a cutter shop for Jillson.[51] Cutter shops cut the corn from the cobs and shipped it to other factories for canning.

Case Study: Strong Sweet Corn

The corn cannery at Strong, Maine, represents a classic example of a shop during the teens and twenties. The facility there had been constructed in the 1880's by Franklin Packing Company, but was soon acquired by Burnham & Morrill and designated their factory #11. Its location in the productive Sandy River Valley and on rail service made it an attractive investment. Agreements between canners and farmers were specific concerning seed to be used, planting, harvesting and pricing (Figure 4.8).

By 1915 this physical plant consisted of the standard complex

Figure 4.7   Corn Shop Crew, Otisfield, Maine, 1912. *Source:* Ephraim
Jillson.

of sheds, processing, packing and warehouse space (Figure 4.9). At this
time much, if not all, of the husking would probably have been done by
hand. There was little need to integrate the husking shed into the more
mechanized aspects of the shop. The husking shed was often a detached
building until canneries fully adopted husking machines. This is also
reflective of the effort to keep child huskers away from machinery and
thus avoid labor law violations.[52] For example, the September 16,
1917 work roster indicates huskers were paid by the basket (piece
work). The low production (less than 12 baskets for the day) of some
of the huskers suggests they may have been children. On the other
hand, seven of the twelve huskers listed received credit for 23-35
baskets.[53] At the going pay rate of that period, five cents per basket (30
x .05) would yield $1.50 a day for a fast worker. Arthur Hill, who
started work in 1918 at age eleven as a hand husker in the Baxter
Brothers shop at Fryeburg, Maine, was paid six cents for each two-
bushel basket. He was paid in husking tokens that had a value set each
year depending on pay scale established by the company. He recalls

It is *hereby agreed*: by and between **Burnham & Morrill** Co. of Portland, in the County of Cumberland, of the one part, and the other subscribers hereto, each for himself that each of the said other subscribers will, during the present season, plant at the proper time with sweet corn, from seed furnished for the current year of 1911 by said Burnham & Morrill Co., the quantity of land, in measured acres, here-under set against his name, and properly cultivate the same and when the corn is in a green and milky condition and suitable for packing, he will notify the agent or attorney of said Burnham & Morrill Co., at their factory in

.... *Strong Maine* ....

and deliver at said factory as ordered, the same to be de-livered in the husks, in the usual and customary manner.

And the said Burnham & Morrill Co., agrees with each of said subscribers to pay him 2 1/2 cents for each and every sixteen ounces of corn, when cut from the cob.

And each of said subscribers hereby agrees that he will not plant any sweet corn seed for canning purposes except the seed furnished by Burnham & Morrill Co., this season. And no corn will be received by Burnham & Morrill Co., ex-cept such as has been raised from seed furnished by them, and in a green and milky condition and suitable for pack-ing; no second picking of corn will be received by said Company; and Burnham & Morrill Co., are to be released from all liability to take the corn, if the factory should be destroyed by fire or other casualty without their fault, provided they by using due diligence are unable to rebuild the factory and procure necessary supplies for packing the corn when in its green and milky condition and suitable for packing.

And each subscriber agrees, if planting any yellow corn whatever, to plant it at a sufficient distance from sweet corn as to prevent any possibility of mixing or chance of the sweet corn being affected by pollen from yellow corn.

Dated this... *Sept. 17* ....A. D. 1910

Burnham & Morrill Co.
Geo Morrill Prest.

Figure 4.8   Agreement. Redrawn from Burnham & Morrill Company Papers, 1910, in the collection of Richard Gould, Farmington, Maine.

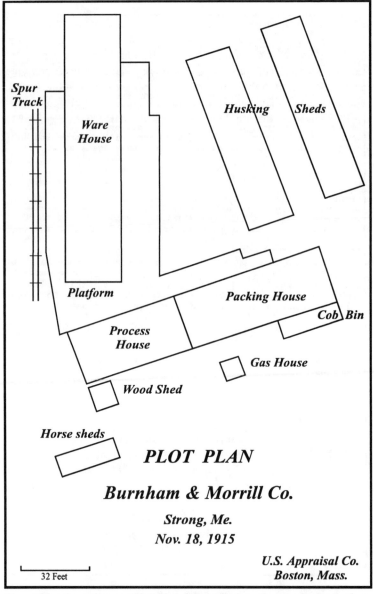

Figure 4.9   Corn Cannery Plot Plan, Strong, Maine. *Source:* Redrawn from
Plot Plan, Burnham & Morrill Company Papers, 1915, in the collection of
Richard Gould, Farmington, Maine.

that the local general store would accept them at company rate.[54]

As demand for canned goods to feed the armed forces grew in the late teens, corn prices shot up. In 1910 Burnham & Morrill paid 2.5 cents per pound of cut corn. A call for more production came from the companies as indicated by the promise of 5 cent corn (Figure 4.10a). Farmers responded by signing up to plant, knowing that war conditions involved uncertain pricing, but in general the market was expected to be sound. Ernest Smith of Phillips agreed to help the war effort by planting three acres (Figure 4.10b).

The Strong corn factory roster for what appears to be 1920 listed 55 employees of whom 33 (60%) were men and 22 (40%) were women. Information on age of workers is not available. The September page for the time book notes that the typical corn shop employee was averaging 11.5 hours per day and working twenty-five days that month. One worker, a Mr. James, put in a 24 hour day followed by a shorter 20 hour shift the next day. He also worked 29 days.[55] When the corn was ready to can, long hours in a rushed environment ensued.

Hourly pay for the individual was not high but the lengthy shifts could yield significant wages at the end of the week. Rose Kennedy received $10.36 for packing and $8.40 for husking for a total of $18.76 in her October 1, 1920 paycheck.[56] Assuming that reflects the period September 24-30, she worked 78 hours for that money and her average hourly rate was $.25.

This combination of incomes from growing corn and shop employment gave a boost to the region's economy. In cases where the farmer grew corn and the wife and possibly children worked in the cannery, the fall could be the highwater mark of household income. Although a few farmers might work at the cornshop, most that planted corn were fully occupied getting it harvested, transported to the shop and taking care of other farm duties. The Strong records reveal that some husbands and wives profited. One couple, Logan and Vera Luce were involved with the Strong shop in the 1920's. In 1926 Logan contracted to plant 1.25 acres of sweet corn and managed to put in 1.1 while Vera (year uncertain but probably 1920) worked as a cutter feeder and box nailer/sealer.[57] In the 1950's the Luces moved 30 miles down the Sandy River to a farm near my home in Starks where they grew corn for the local factory and Vera worked in the shop during the canning season. Logan and I sometimes picked corn together as part of the harvest crew on the Frederic farm.

TO THE PLANTER OF SWEET CORN FOR
BURNHAM & MORRILL COMPANY
   Uncle Sam urges that all planters make a special effort to raise large crops.
   We must feed our Boys in France and help feed the Allies.
   Sweet corn is a staple food that is used by the Army and the Navy.
   ARE YOU DOING YOUR SHARE TO HELP THE BOYS AT THE FRONT?
   We are paying 5¢ per pound for Sweet Corn this year to encourage planting. Plant all you can.
   The women of England and France are doing the farming. Are not the women of America equally able to assist in this necessary work? See our Superintendent and sign up for all the Sweet Corn you can plant.

                                        Yours truly,

                                        BURHHAM & MORRILL COMPANY

Figure 4.10a   Call for More Corn - Request for Corn. *Source:* Redrawn from Burnham & Morrill Company Papers, 1918, in the collection of Richard Gould, Farmington, Maine.

THIS IS NOT A CONTRACT OR A PLEDGE
To The Planter of Sweet Corn:
       As a matter of co-operation we desire to ask you how much Sweet Corn you will consider planting for us in 1918. If you intend to plant any we urge you to prepare your land this fall.
       Owing to the uncertainty as to the duration of the war and the present erratic condition of the market we are unable to make a price for Sweet Corn today but assure you that when the price is made by us it will be a fair and just one. We do not consider it fair to the planter or ourselves to make a price now but will do so next spring when acerage books will be put out. In the meantime it will be helpful to us to have an estimate of what is in prospect. We therefore ask you to enter on this slip the number of acres you will plant provided conditions are favorable and the price is right.

   __3__ Acres

       Sign here *Ernest Smith*

       P.O. Address *Phillips, Maine*

Figure 4.10b   Call for More Corn - Intent to Plant. *Source:* Redrawn from Burnham & Morrill Company Papers, 1918, in the collection of Richard Gould, Farmington, Maine.

In 1926 eighty-nine farmers contracted to grow 214 acres of sweet corn for the Burnham & Morrill shop in Strong. Of these, eighty-eight planted 205.10 acres; ninety-nine percent of the contractors with ninety-six percent of the promised acreage. This is a good indication of how seriously growers honored their agreement with the companies and a reflection of their interest in cash. An average of 2.33 acres per farm suggests that few depended on sweet corn for a large part of their income. Only two producers put in 10 or more acres and twenty-four percent had an acre or less.[58] Hand labor and slow horse drawn equipment was still the norm. Farmers knew that too much corn would result in problems from weeds to not picking on time.

The Strong shop had been constructed on the narrow gauge (2 foot) railroad line that connected northern Franklin County to the standard gauge at Farmington (Figure 4.11). This transportation infrastructure made it possible for the cannery to draw its supply of raw material from more than the few miles surrounding its location. An examination of addresses of growers and their acreage documents that about sixty percent of the farmers and acreage were in Strong. Approximately twenty percent of farmers and production were in the Phillips community (10 miles away) and fifteen percent of the acreage was in Farmington, which had several canneries at the time. My knowledge of names of those Farmington farmers shipping to Strong (some are my relatives) and their general geographic concentration in the northern part of Farmington suggests they took advantage of the narrow gauge that passed near their properties. Smaller tonnage was sent from Salem and Kingfield, the latter nearly twenty miles away. Farmers in Avon and Freeman undoubtedly grew for the corn shop but those communities had no post office and their addresses would have been Strong, Salem or Kingfield for Freeman and Phillips or Strong for Avon. No farmers with a New Vineyard address grew for the cannery. That community had its own post office but no rail link to Strong. In addition, mountainous terrain between the two towns made road transport difficult. The Strong shop had a far greater spatial impact than most canneries of the period. Transportation was one key to success.

Competition From Other Sweet Corn Canning Regions

Although detailed statistics on national corn pack are not available for the nineteenth century, spotty numbers indicate that Northern New

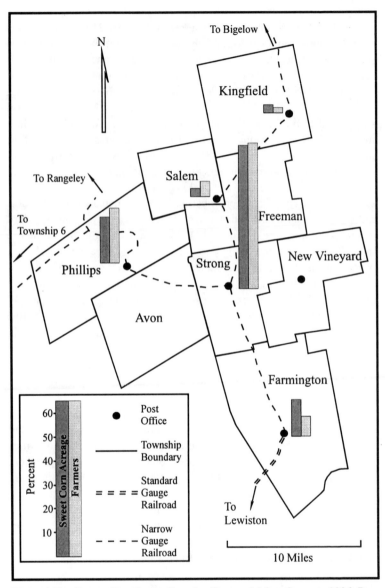

Figure 4.11   Sweet Corn Production for Strong, Maine, Cannery, 1926: Percentage of Farmers and Acreage by Postal Address. *Source*: Burnham & Morrill Company Paper, in the collection of Richard Gould, Farmington, Maine; compiled by author.

England produced more than half of all canned corn at that time. According to a paper delivered before the Maine Canners Association in 1958:

> ...in the early 1900's, this young industry took Horace Greeley's advice and went West... Gradually, Maine's share of the market slacked from 100% in early days, until in 1920 we produced only about 12% of the total packed, but this was still far more than Wisconsin and Minnesota combined.[59]

Sweet corn was, by no means, the first agricultural product to find its way West from Northern New England. This theme is constant throughout Wilson's detailed work, *The Hill Country of Northern New England.* "Montana and Wyoming, marauding giants have reached across the continent and stolen our 'beef critters',... Minnesota and Iowa have sown tares amongst our wheat."[60] By 1930 the West had not pushed Maine, New Hampshire and Vermont out of the sweet corn business, but competition was being felt by its canners. According to 1930 data, five states were growing more sweet corn for processing than all of Northern New England. Illinois was leading with 75,000 acres (Table 4.4). Although crop value data are not published for all states, figures are available for the leading canned corn areas. In 1920, Maine ranked third behind Illinois and Iowa in value of sweet corn grown for canning (Table 4.5). Ten years later the state was still third. Number of acres planted to sweet corn is not an exact indication of raw corn production or value of the crop because yield per acre differs greatly from one state to another (Table 4.6 and Table 4.7). Maine and New Hampshire led the United States in sweet corn yield per acre in 1920. Data for 1930 show Maine having a yield of 3.7 tons per acre and New Hampshire having an average of 3.0. The national average was only 1.76 tons per acre. This great difference in production of raw sweet corn per acre is one of the factors contributing to the continued growth of the industry in Northern New England during the 1920's. Higher prices for raw corn also aided growers of Maine, New Hampshire and Vermont in maintaining a competitive position in the face of increasing western production. Maine and New Hampshire also led the nation in price paid for raw sweet corn in 1920 (Table 4.8). Maine farmers received $30.00 a ton for raw sweet corn that year and New Hampshire growers were paid $25.00 compared to the country's average of $19.32. Maryland,

	1920	1930	1940	1950	1960	1965
Maine	15,820	13,440	8,600	6,600	3,000	1,300
New Hampshire	68	1,110	420	350	a	a
Vermont	2,140	2,140	1,190	630	a	a
Delaware	3,000	3,700	2,000	3,800	5,000	3,300
Idaho	a	a	3,000	7,700	12,500	16,400
Illinois	48,540	75,000	54,000	55,000	63,900	54,200
Indiana	10,580	44,280	48,900	21,000	a	a
Iowa	55,850	56,000	24,500	17,000	5,500	5,900
Maryland	24,590	46,200	30,200	27,900	30,800	29,200
Michigan	6,950	12,400	2,800	1,700	a	a
Minnesota	11,860	54,330	53,400	65,300	95,000	103,800
Nebraska	7,490	8,000	2,900	750	a	a
New York	27,070	26,200	22,300	23,800	20,400	14,000
Ohio	30,970	38,000	20,700	9,800	a	a
Oregon	a	a	1,500	21,900	21,900	30,500
Pennsylvania	3,430	7,500	11,900	10,500	9,100	9,500
Tennessee	a	3,400	a	a	a	a
Utah	a	a	550	4,900	a	a
Virginia	a	a	500	500	a	a
Washington	a	a	3,900	9,600	22,700	21,500
Wisconsin	10,870	14,500	32,900	73,000	104,000	114,600
Other States	1,910	4,140	8,390	8,800	36,700	16,450
Total	261,750	410,400	334,570	358,130	430,700	430,650

Table 4.4   Sweet Corn Acreage Planted for Processing. *Source:* U.S.D.A. *Vegetable Statistics,* 1928, Table 13; *Commercial Vegetables,* 1953, 59-67; *Vegetables for Processing,* 1967, Table 8; [a] included in other states.

	1920	1930	1940	1950	1960	1965
Maine	1,470	1,283	415	394	339	144
New Hampshire	48	74	17	20	a	a
Vermont	94	85	26	40	a	a
Delaware	84	84	38	225	317	258
Idaho	a	a	47	559	1,308	1,912
Illinois	2,109	1,872	920	2,788	4,267	4,843
Indiana	488	747	451	465	a	a
Iowa	2,005	1,155	389	682	285	355
Maryland	1,470	345	601	1,049	1,984	2,121
Michigan	201	57	32	35	a	a
Minnesota	444	1,348	1,495	3,444	4,549	7,644
Nebraska	185	108	39	20	a	a
New York	1,205	502	324	1,594	1,565	1,412
Ohio	1,156	405	323	393	a	a
Oregon	a	a	70	937	2,543	4,039
Pennsylvania	128	109	270	530	673	517
Tennessee	a	103	a	a	a	a
Utah	a	a	29	332	a	a
Virginia	a	a	12	24	a	a
Washington	a	a	163	768	2,262	3,921
Wisconsin	336	346	750	2,351	4,496	7,632
Other States	80	119	192	554	2,180	1,341
Total	11,503	8,742	6,512	17,204	26,768	36,159

Table 4.5   Farm Value of Sweet Corn Crop for Processing, Thousand of Dollars. *Source:* U.S.D.A. *Vegetable Statistics,* 1928; *Commercial Vegetables,* 1953, 59-67; *Vegetables For Processing,* 1967, Table 8; [a] included in Other States.

	1920	1930	1940	1950	1960	1965
Maine	49,000	48,800	27,100	20,400	14,200	6,700
New Hampshire	1,900	3,200	1,200	1,000	a	a
Vermont	4,700	4,800	2,500	2,100	a	a
Delaware	5,400	6,500	4,000	11,500	16,700	10,800
Idaho	a	a	6,000	31,400	61,700	84,600
Illinois	106,800	144,000	110,800	154,900	216,600	205,200
Indiana	26,400	56,600	53,100	30,600	a	a
Iowa	128,500	110,000	59,000	37,900	17,400	21,500
Maryland	63,900	23,800	62,600	66,800	99,700	91,800
Michigan	13,900	4,400	2,900	2,200	a	a
Minnesota	29,600	129,600	186,900	202,600	275,700	353,200
Nebraska	15,000	10,800	5,800	1,400	a	a
New York	54,100	29,900	36,800	78,500	70,200	53,100
Ohio	61,900	35,800	29,800	26,900	a	a
Oregon	a	a	5,000	33,700	106,400	167,600
Pennsylvania	7,500	6,800	25,500	26,500	29,400	23,700
Tennessee	a	6,800	a	a	a	a
Utah	a	a	2,500	17,300	a	a
Virginia	a	a	1,000	1,600	a	a
Washington	a	a	16,000	40,000	105,700	158,100
Wisconsin	21,700	31,200	80,600	146,000	262,900	368,700
Other States	5,000	8,400	19,000	24,800	114,360	68,600
U.S. Total	595,000	661,440	738,000	958,000	1,390,960	1,613,600

Table 4.6   Raw Sweet Corn Production, Tons in Husk. *Source:* U.S.D.A. *Vegetable Statistics,*1928,Table 13; *Commercial Vegetables,*1953, 59-67; *Vegetables for Processing,* 1967, Table 8; [a] included in Other States.

	1920	1930	1940	1950	1960	1965
Maine	3.1	3.7	3.3	3.4	4.72	5.15
New Hampshire	2.8	3.0	3.5	3.0	NA	NA
Vermont	2.2	2.3	2.7	3.5	NA	NA
Delaware	1.8	1.8	2.0	3.1	3.40	3.38
Idaho	a	a	2.0	4.3	5.02	6.31
Illinois	2.2	2.0	2.1	2.9	3.46	4.23
Indiana	2.5	1.3	1.1	1.5	a	a
Iowa	3.3	2.0	2.5	2.4	3.35	4.13
Maryland	2.6	.7	2.1	2.5	3.30	3.22
Michigan	2.0	.6	1.2	2.0	a	a
Minnesota	2.5	2.4	3.5	3.3	3.02	3.86
Nebraska	2.0	1.4	2.0	2.0	a	3.38
New York	2.0	1.3	2.1	3.4	3.53	4.05
Ohio	2.0	1.1	1.6	2.8	a	a
Oregon	a	a	3.3	4.95	4.95	5.82
Pennsylvania	2.2	.9	2.1	2.6	3.30	2.58
Tennessee	a	2.0	a	a	a	a
Utah	a	a	5.0	3.6	a	a
Virginia	a	a	2.0	3.3	a	a
Washington	a	a	4.2	4.4	4.76	5.20
Wisconsin	2.0	2.4	2.6	2.3	2.75	4.19
Other States	2.6	2.2	2.4	2.9	3.34	4.40
Average	2.3	1.76	2.3	2.85	3.31	4.28

Table 4.7   Sweet Corn Yield Per Acre in Tons. *Source:* U.S.D.A. *Vegetable Statistics,*1928, Table 13; *Commercial Vegetables,* 1953, 59-67; *Vegetables for Processing,*1967, Table 8; [a] included in Other States.

	1920	1930	1940	1950	1960	1965
Maine	$30.00	$26.30	$15.30	$19.30	$23.90	$21.50
New Hampshire	25.00	23.10	14.20	20.00	a	a
Vermont	20.00	17.70	10.30	19.00	a	a
Delaware	15.60	13.00	9.50	19.60	19.00	23.90
Idaho	a	a	7.80	17.80	21.20	22.60
Illinois	17.75	13.00	8.30	18.00	19.70	23.60
Indiana	18.50	13.20	8.50	15.20	a	a
Iowa	15.60	10.50	6.60	18.00	16.40	16.50
Maryland	23.00	14.00	9.60	15.70	19.90	23.10
Michigan	14.46	13.00	11.00	16.00	a	a
Minnesota	15.00	10.40	8.00	17.00	16.50	21.70
Nebraska	12.33	10.00	6.70	14.00	a	a
New York	22.28	16.80	8.80	20.30	22.30	26.60
Ohio	18.67	11.30	7.80	14.60	a	a
Oregon	a	a	13.90	27.80	23.90	24.10
Pennsylvania	17.00	16.00	10.60	20	22.90	21.80
Tennessee	a	15.10	a	a	a	a
Utah	a	a	11.60	19.20	a	a
Virginia	a	a	12.00	14.70	a	a
Washington	a	a	10.20	19.20	21.40	24.80
Wisconsin	15.50	11.10	9.30	16.10	17.10	20.70
Other States	15.91	14.17	10.10	22.00	19.06	19.55
Average	19.32	13.22	8.82	18.00	19.94	22.41

Table 4.8   Sweet Corn Price Per Ton in Husk. *Source:* U.S.D.A. *Vegetable Statistics,* 1928, Table 13; *Commercial Vegetables,* 1953, 59-67; *Vegetables for Processing,* 1967; [a]included in Other States.

New York and Vermont were the only other states where prices were $20.00 or more. A decade later, in 1930, sweet corn prices had dropped somewhat as a result of the economic depression that was just starting. Maine and New Hampshire still maintained their price lead by large margins. Farmers in these two states were receiving $26.30 and $23.10 respectively while those in Nebraska and Iowa were being paid only $10.00 and $10.50 per ton of sweet corn. The higher prices paid for sweet corn grown in Northern New England reflect the consumer attitude toward corn processed in that area. During the late 1800's and early 1900's, Maine had built a reputation for producing high quality Crosby corn, and this carried through the 20's in the face of western production. The western corn canners attempted to improve their pack by using seed and machinery developed in the East along with their own innovations. Frank W. Douthitt did as much as anyone to improve the quality of western sweet corn. According to Earl May in *The Canning Clan*:

In 1911... Douthitt secured a U.S. Patent of Bantam (Golden Bantam)... he, the first to secure Crosby seed from Maine, can it in Western Territory and sell it in competition with Maine canners, was also the first to secure a trade-mark for a deep yellow strain of canning corn. Adding one more claim to advantageous achievement he put out Whole Kernel Bantam corn commercially, in advance of competition and invented machinery with which to can it.[61]

As a result of these and other developments in the agricultural West, Northern New England could not hope to maintain control of the canned corn market. One of the earliest accounts that indicate rising concern among New England processors appears in Bert Fernald's work of 1902. He points out that as of that year:

In the packing of corn, Maine stands third in quantity and first in quality, New York ranking first in quantity and Illinois second...Our farmers, as well as canned corn packers, have suffered untold wrongs and lost thousands of dollars by unscrupulous packers in the West, who have packed inferior goods there, and sold them under a "State of Maine" label and it is the opinion of those best informed that many more goods were packed outside the state and sold for Maine corn than were [sic] packed in the state, thus bringing reproach to our products, and forcing the price to an almost profitless business, for both farmer and packer. The western states are increasing their pack yearly, and it is only the superior quality and flavor of Maine sweet corn that enables the packers here to maintain themselves against the powerful competition of the corn states.[62]

He appears to follow his own advice. As a partner in the corn canning company, Fernald, Keene and True, he made profits that helped propel him to the Governorship and U.S. Senate. Northern New England growers and processors answered his challenge, but not with total success. Many companies emphasized "Maine Corn" on their labels and promoted the concept of rural purity (Figure 4.12). What is more idyllic than a group of well dressed children picking wild flowers on the bank of a stream? Reality suggests that a more common scene would be finding them picking corn or working in a cannery! Steps were taken to maintain a high quality product, but these efforts only slowed rather than stopped the encroachment of western corn into eastern markets. Breeding programs and improved canning methods were developed in the three state areas, but many of these gains were offset by western innovations. One factor that helped Maine, New Hampshire,

Figure 4.12   Maine Corn. *Source:* Author.

and Vermont hold an edge in quality was the difference in contracting methods between the West and these three states. This is one of the basic theories that L.V. Burton presents in his work, "'Corn Shops' Down in Maine."

> Many ... regions purchase sweet corn on the ear at a flat rate per ton, but not so in Maine. Here the practice is to pay on the basis of the amount of cut corn that can be obtained from a sample take from the load and further the price usually varies with the quality of the sample. But back of all this is the fact that the methods of harvesting in Maine are entirely different from those which are employed in the Middlewest. In Illinois, ..., when the field man says it is time to harvest a given field of corn, it is picked clean. The field man's decision as to when to pick the field is based on the average condition of the crop. If any sorting of the ears is to be made to segregate different degrees of maturity, that sorting is done on belts in the factory. Old mature ears and young blisters are thrown out. The success of this method depends largely on the uniformity of the crop. It also means that plantings must be made successively so that harvesting can also be made successively.
>
> In Maine, however, cornfields are picked over several times, each

picking being made with the idea of getting only the ears that, ... are at the right stage of maturity for canning. Thus, the system of purchase based on a rate per pound of cut kernels, depending on the quality, is an incentive to a farmer to bring in the crop at its ideal stage. Many of the Maine corn shops have small laboratory-like cutting departments in which the test is made, the weight of cut kernels obtained, and the rate of pay fixed.[63]

Between 1880 and 1930 Northern New England experienced tremendous growth within the sweet corn industry. Canneries had spread from a small cluster in Maine into New Hampshire and Vermont. The region had built a reputation for its quality pack which resulted from the physical environments to which Crosby corn was adapted, and contracting and canning methods that insured a product with high sugar content. Canners and planters had disagreed at times during this era, but by 1930 the differences were pretty well resolved. New processing machinery and methods were introduced in great numbers. The streamlining of shops increased production while reducing the required number of workers. Plant breeding programs by private and public organizations resulted in sweet corn strains with greater yields and more uniformity. Mechanical and tilling innovations on farms resulted in increased yield and greater ease in producing the raw product. Motor trucks enabled canneries to serve more farms and increasingly larger areas.

This half-century also saw the West rise as a giant sweet corn canner and competitor. As transportation facilities between the western producing areas and the large eastern markets improved, the advantage of nearness to the consumers that Northern New England held began to decline. Sweet corn hybrids adapted to the Midwest, and the ability to utilize mechanical innovations to cope with the relatively short harvest period when the corn kernels had a high sugar content, enabled these canners to improve quality as they increased output. In 1930 Northern New England was still one of the leading gold canning regions of the country, but its position was being challenged by states to the west.

Chapter 5

Decline of the Industry, 1931 - 1968

Between 1931 and 1968 the sweet corn canning industry in Northern New England declined until only one corn shop was left and in 1969 none canned gold. Innovations in corn canning and related businesses could not reverse this trend.

Reduction of Corn Canning Operations

The corn processing business may be measured in several ways. Canning establishments, pack, value of crop and acreage are reliable indicators of patterns within the industry. Corn shops, which numbered one-hundred and nine in 1930, disappeared. The depression decade of 1930-1940 experienced a significant reduction in plants. During these years, smaller operations were the hardest hit, although all canners suffered to a certain extent. Small companies find it much more difficult to absorb losses over a series of bad years than do larger concerns with greater working capital. Black points out that:

> The acreage of sweet corn ... fluctuates violently from year to year; and the canning output still more so. Under the system of contracting for the desired acreage, it is possible for the processors to reduce the crop whenever an unusual yield or decline in consumption has built up their stocks to abnormal levels. They resort to this practice freely. The 1935 national pack of sweet corn was 21.5 million cases, that of 1936 was down to 14.6 million, and that of 1937 was up to 23.4 million. The New England production has a pattern somewhat of its own depending on supplies of its particular types.[1]

L. P. True and Company of Hope, Maine, is one example of a small operation that could not withstand these fluctuations in the economic cycle. This company began canning corn about 1870. During its early years all of the corn was husked and cut by hand with a Winslow corn knife. Around 1915 custom canning became a major aspect of the business. This service involved canning for individuals who were not contract growers, but who desired to have produce cannned for resale or for their own use. Smaller operations were inclined to take these orders whereas larger canneries were less likely to engage in such activity. Later string beans, tomatoes, apples, squash, and blueberries were packed in small quantities. The plant managed to withstand the first few years of the Depression but by 1937 conditions were such that it had to stop operating. The last few years it canned, the place was powered by a four-cylinder Chevrolet car engine.[2] Pressure on the industry continued; "Owing to a tremendous carryover into the 1939 season, only approximately one-third of the corn factories in Maine operated..."[3]

Despite the reduction of corn canners, drop in price per ton, value of the crop, pack and raw sweet corn production, the crop continued to play an important role in the rural economy during the Depression. Day, states that in 1940:

> Corn was the principal vegetable,... More sweet corn was grown on the fertile and extensive intervals along the Saco River in Fryeburg than in any other equal area in the state... On a few farms around Farmington and Fryeburg, sweet corn was the principal cash crop, but on most farms it was grown as a supplement enterprise to dairying... The leading variety was Golden Bantam, although White Crosby, once popular, was still grown to a certain extent.[4]

Between 1940 and 1950 the number of factories decreased from eighty-two to sixty-three (Table 4.1). The small operations such as George F. Hinds of Livermore, J. W. Pratt Company of Farmington, Kennebec Valley Canning Company in Solon, and Thomas and Marble of Wilton (all in Maine), were forced out of business. Frederick Payne, the third governor involved with corn canning, leased the Pratt shop at its end.[5] Even the magic touch of politicans couldn't save the day. In addition to its Portland plant, the Burnham & Morrill Company operated ten canning factories in 1950; packing string beans, squash and blueberries in addition to sweet corn. Canning season at these plants stretched across a two-month period.[6] H. C. Baxter and Brothers,

Portland Packing Company and Monmouth Canning Company owned twenty-seven of the fifty-three other corn shops.[7] Undoubtedly the demands of the Second World War slowed the decline of the industry during the 40's.

Forty-four corn shops went out of business in Northern New England between 1950 and 1960. Of the nineteen remaining plants, only the one at Starks processed just sweet corn. This is evidence of an attempt to spread the economic risk among several different products, such as beans and blueberries. Small operations such as George H. Hall and Sons of Dexter, Maine, and Green Mountain Packing Company of Saint Albans, Vermont, were most likely to go out of business during these years. In addition to family companies, the much larger Portland Packing Company sold out. Some of the canning plants operated by Portland Packing were purchased, while others were closed, never to open again. Monmouth Canning Company acquired Portland Packing's Canton, Maine, plant in 1955.[8] Some companies such as H. L. Forhan discontinued sweet corn canning, but continued processing blueberries or other products.[9]

Over the years fire took its toll of shops. While attending secondary school at New Sharon, Maine, I witnessed the spectacular destruction of the Medomak Canning Company plant in that community. It was November 1960, and the factory warehouse section was packed with canned goods ready for labels and shipping to market. The fire started in the night and was well underway before an alarm could be sounded. By the time pumpers and firefighters arrived, flames were widespread and super heated sealed cans of corn, beans, squash, etc. were exploding with skyrocket results. Fire chief Frank Brown ordered his men to stay clear of the building and remain out of can range, which was greater than that of fire hoses, until the hot vegetable barrage subsided. By then the shop was reduced to ashes.[10] Ina Tuner, a regular seasonal worker, who lived five miles away, could hear cans bursting and see smoke and remarked, "Oh, what will we do now? What will we do next year? The cannery is gone!"[11] During this period of decline, when a corn canning plant closed or was destroyed, its fate was usually final, never to be operated again. The factory was the major industry within this small town and its loss had considerable impact upon the local economy. Sweet corn, string beans, and squash could no longer be grown as cash crops by the farmers, seasonal employment was not available, a few year-round jobs were lost and a large source of tax revenue for the town was removed as a result of the fire. Local citizens expressed their concern by forming a committee to try to get the plant rebuilt, but the Medomak owners felt such action would not be economically sound.

Between 1960 and 1967 corn canneries continued to decline in number and by autumn of the latter year only the A. L. Stewart and Son plant at Freedom, Maine, canned corn. During these seven years Burnham & Morrill became a subsidiary of the William Underwood Company of Boston, and abandoned its sweet corn operations; H. C. Baxter and Brothers ceased canning corn; the Monmouth Canning Company sold its canning interests to A. L. Stewart and Son and the leading Vermont canner, Demeritt Company, stopped processing. None of the long established sweet corn canners were operating. The A. L. Stewart and Son Company had been primarily concerned with blueberry processing, although during the mid-fifties it had attempted sweet corn at Dexter. The 1967 season was the first time in about ten years that Stewart canned corn and none was packed after that one year. Although the Franklin Farms shop in Farmington did not can in 1967, its owner, Richard Gould, leased the plant to Collins Foods of Connecticut for the 1968 season and corn was canned. Collins did not renew the lease for a second year. Thus, the last corn shop to operate in the three-state region closed forever.

Karl Soule considers the primary factors contributing to closure of the corn canneries: (1) The availability of the raw product is not so great as in past years because farmers declined to grow sweet corn as much as they did in earlier days. (2) The availability of seasonal labor caused considerable problems. The nearer to a milltown a plant was located, the greater the difficulty to get seasonal help. The increasing need for ready cash throughout the year forced seasonal labor out. Freedom was the only plant to operate in 1967 but there is no milltown near Freedom. (3) The plants that process only one product could not compete with shops processing several vegetables. Starks is an example of a one-product plant that went under.[12]

Attempts were made to combat the three problems. Some of the reduction in farm acreage was offset by the increased tendency for many of the companies to grow their own sweet corn. During its last year of operation only three or four farmers grew corn for the Starks shop. Most of the corn canned there was produced on land either owned or leased by the Monmouth Canning Company. Diversification by adding other products was undertaken by most firms, but like sweet corn, a large portion of these crops was grown by the canners rather than the farmers. In some cases part of the labor problem was met by the company supplying worker transportation to the plant during canning season. This resulted in the labor force being drawn from a larger area surrounding the shop. These efforts met with limited success.

Corn acreage dropped until 1939. Only Oxford County had more than 1,250 acres planted to sweet corn, although many counties grew over 250 acres. In light of the general economic conditions of the time this pattern was expected. Most of the canneries that were operating in 1939 were processing at reduced scale. By 1949 acreage indicates that the industry had recovered from the depression of the 1930's but had not reached its 1929 peak. Somerset County edged out Oxford as the leader in sweet corn acreage (Table 4.3). In addition to the two leading areas, Androscoggin, Franklin, Kennebec, Penobscot and Waldo Counties were growing over 750 acres. Although there was an overall reduction of land in sweet corn during the ten years following 1949, Oxford and Somerset were still the leading areas. None of the other counties planted as much as 750 acres in 1959. From the early 1900's until the late 1950's the two major sweet corn producing areas had been Oxford County and Central Maine, consisting of Androscoggin, Kennebec, and Waldo Counties and the southern portions of Franklin, Somerset and Penobscot Counties. In a 1956 study, Hugh J. Murphy compares these two areas in terms of sweet corn production.

> In comparing the Fryeburg area (Oxford County) with the Central Maine area, soils in the latter are generally slightly higher in acidity and somewhat higher in overall fertility as determined by soils analysis. Nevertheless, the better yields in the Fryeburg area approach the better yields in Central Maine. This may be due to superior cultural practices, soil conditions or seeding practices which are common to the area.[13]

During the early 1960's the Oxford County region apparently retained a firmer hold on the industry than did Central Maine. Oxford, Cumberland and Penobscot Counties were the only ones with 250 or more acres of sweet corn in Maine in 1964. Hillsborough and Rockingham Counties, New Hampshire, also grew over 250 acres. Only the corn factory in Pittsfield was operating in New Hampshire during the middle 1960's, and most of this crop probably went into the fresh market of southern New England. For the first time since the United

States Department of Agriculture began reporting sweet corn acreage, Vermont did not have a county growing 250 acres of the crop.

Sweet corn pack varied greatly from year to year, depending on supply and demand. Beginning with the depression years of the 30's the general trend was a reduction of Northern New England sweet corn production. By 1960, Maine, New Hampshire and Vermont pack totaled only 603,000 cases of twenty-four number 303 cans (Table 4.2).

Canning Innovations

New ideas continued to change the nature of crop production and processing. Most of the packing was now done in well appointed buildings designed to accommodate new equipment and many of the smaller, less efficient operations had ceased production (Figure 5.1). Corn canning had become a relatively smooth flowing process (Figure 5.2). Conveyor chains and belts moved material from place to place in the shops (Figure 5.3). Machines replaced hand husking and hand cutting (Figure 5.4). Improvements were made in washing, desilking and mixing equipment (Figure 5.5). Cold pack with handmade cans was replaced by pouring hot corn into mass produced cans purchased from a can company and capped by an automatic sealer (Figure 5.6). Carefully controlled retorts made possible a well cooked, safe final product. Government inspection programs directed at food quality standards expanded and canneries were subject to additional visits. Most of these new inventions were associated with reducing labor and streamlining production. Both factory and field operations were influenced by this trend. In an article reporting on the Freedom, Maine, plant, Ramsey points out that:

> Hand harvesting no longer exists in the corn and bean fields ... plants ... must be highly mechanized to compete in a world where economy is in a constant state of transition. Labor costs have been the downfall of many canneries...[14]

Figure 5.1   Corn Shop Country. This photograph taken between 1932 and 1936 illustrates the role of the canning industry in the Sandy River Valley of Maine. At this time four corn shops were operating in Farmington Village; Franklin Farms Products (long white building in foreground), Pratt (center-right), Burnham & Morrill and Edward Marble (both to the left out of view). Although a number of hill farms continued to grow sweet corn, the abundant acreage of fertile floodplain gave the region an advantage. Rail service (rail yard next to Pratt shop) was also advantageous. Franklin Farms had built a modern plant following a 1932 fire while the Pratt facility is representative of small older operations that had difficulty staying competitive. The critical need to be close to water is also evident. In 1936 the river cut off the meander (note soon to be main channel at left), leaving the two shops with the problem of getting their waste to flowing water. Pratts closed soon after World War Two while the last corn canned in Maine (1968) came from the Franklin Farms building, then leased by Collins Foods. *Source:* Richard Gould, Farmington, Maine.

88 *Canning Gold*

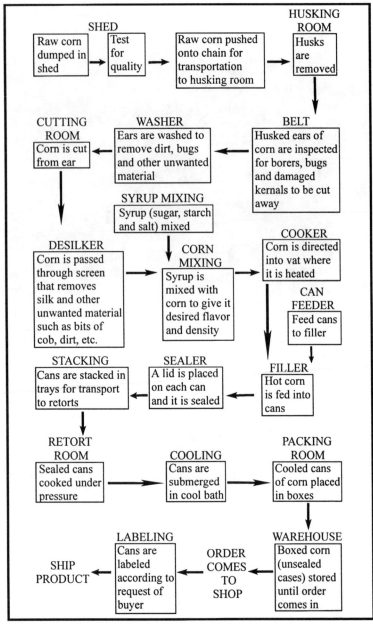

Figure 5.2   Canning Corn, Post-World War One.

Figure 5.3   Hoeing Corn into Conveyor Chain, about 1950. *Source:* Richard Gould.

Figure 5.4   Double Husking Machine, about 1950. *Source:* Richard Gould.

Figure 5.5   Feeding Corn Mixer, about 1950. *Source*: Richard Gould.

Figure 5.6   Filling Cans, about 1950. *Source*: Richard Gould.

L.V. Burton argues that developments in the canning industry arise from two major sources:

(1) The economic necessity of securing a lower unit cost for overhead by putting a larger volume through the plant without materially increasing the fixed investment;

(2) The necessity of adapting the style of output to the demands of the trade.[15]

With maximum profits in mind corn canners continually adopted innovations during the years between 1931 and 1968. Some of these did not prove economically sound in the long run, whereas others were more significant in slowing the industry's regional decline. Although the basic principles of canning did not change during this era, much of the canning equipment was modified to increase speed. Undoubtedly this streamlining process resulted in the closure of many of the small companies that did not have the venture capital to purchase or lease expensive pieces of machinery.

In addition to the efficient processing equipment, the so-called "cutting shop" was more widely used during the 1930's. These shops were the result of an effort by many New England canners to increase production at the larger canning factories. Older small plants were used as cutting stations and a few cutting shops were built in outlying areas. Their primary function was to husk and silk the corn, cut it from the cobs, and ship it to central shops for canning. John Gould describes one of the problems of getting cut corn to the canning shop (Figure 5.7).

The word 'cream' is misleading. When our Maine kind of yellow sweet corn was cut from the cobs, the natural juices of the kernels quickly took on a milky appearance, but there was never any cream added. The sugar content went into a chemical change almost immediately, making it necessary to get the product sealed into the cans fast. This was the principal reason for having so many scattered corn shops close to the fields; another reason was the great bulk of the waste material. There was no point in transporting cobs and husks to a distant corn shop when only the golden kernels were to be used. The old Burnham & Morrill tried to tighten up costs one time and got into an amusing employee situation.

They decided to cut the corn as the local farmers brought it in, and then truck the milky kernels to their main plant at Portland for the closing operation and the time in the retorts. They bought a great parcel of 40-

quart milk cans which were filled with the kernels, and as fast as a truckload was ready they'd race to Portland. Because the natural enzymes began at once to labor and perform, the covers on these cans, which were merely great tin stoppers, were hammered down for the trip.

By the time the truck got to Portland the milky contents had already built up enough fermentation gas so the cans were almost bombs. The technicians decided things hadn't gone far enough to reduce the quality of the tinned corn, but the workmen had the job of removing the covers. A wooden mallet was used to strike up under the edges of the covers, and then as each was loosened it would blow sky-high. The B & M corn operation, while thus consolidated into a less expensive payroll, now had to hire an extra man whose job was to run about like a baseball outfielder and catch covers when they came down.[16]

According to Burton the greatest problem facing this type of operation was maintaining a high sugar content in the corn during its transportation from the "cutting shop" to the cannery. Attempts to keep the cut corn cool by packing it in ice proved to be expensive. After a

Figure 5.7   Corn Bomb. *Source: Christian Science Monitor.*

period of several years this method of operation was abandoned by most of the companies that had adopted it.[17]

Plant Breeding Innovations

As adjustments were being undertaken in the cannery, sweet corn varieties were also improved. During the 1930's and 40's, "...the sweet corn breeders ... channeled their efforts into two general types-one of which is used as canning and the other of which is best adapted for roasting on the ear..."[18] The rise of Golden Bantam as the major canning corn caused an increase in experimentation with this variety. May points out that "a million pounds of Golden Bantam seed went out to growers in 1935 for commercial production. In 1936, 35,000 acres of Golden Bantam were grown where only white had grown before."[19] The decline of the white types of sweet corn was nationwide. By 1950 the white varieties were absent from the three Northern New England states (Table 5.1).

The University of Maine Experiment Station at Monmouth expanded its sweet corn breeding program under Russell Bailey. By the mid-1930's the so-called "Maine 100" had been developed as a result of work with some of the locally adapted Golden Bantam strains. Yields from this new plant were from ten to twenty percent greater than the old open pollinated types. Because Maine canners became interested in using "Maine 100" in their canning, a seed program was undertaken. Each following year several thousand pounds of this seed were grown in the state. This increased yield succeeded, to a certain extent, in meeting competition from other sweet corn producing areas. As time went on, other hybrids such as Dirigo, Hybrid-C and Maine Tri-Cross were developed as canning strains. Most of these were produced in the western part of the state under the direction of Maine Canner's Seed Company and the Agricultural Experimental Station. In time it was found that seed production in Northern New England was hazardous. With the increased introduction of hybrid lines, it was often difficult to get the seed to mature fully, and this sometimes resulted in small poor quality seed. As a result, beginning in 1944 the Maine Canner's Seed Company gave up seed production in the state and contracted with Idaho seed producers to supply their needs. The Idaho area could produce better seed because it was irrigated, and excellent parent seed could be maintained there due to its isolation. Many of the hybrids

	1930		1935		1940		1945		1950	
	White	Yellow	White	Yellow	White	Yellow	White	Yellow	White	Yellow
Maine	3,740	6,950	3,160	12,660	690	7,910	920	12,280	-	6,600
New Hampshire	250	700	220	780	50	370	-	450	-	350
Vermont	250	1,090	-	1,240	1,190	1,190	-	1,030	-	630
Delaware	3,400	-	2,800	-	1,000	1,000	-	4,200	1,600	2,200
Idaho	-	-	-	940	180	2,820	-	7,100	-	7,700
Illinois	60,350	10,650	60,450	32,550	25,920	28,080	23,500	45,600	24,750	30,250
Indiana	39,900	2,110	39,000	11,000	13,200	13,200	15,600	24,400	18,690	2,310
Iowa	53,800	1,100	43,500	6,500	17,880	6,620	27,440	24,960	1,190	15,810
Maryland	40,200	-	31,050	3,450	17,510	12,690	18,570	24,630	6,700	21,200
Michigan	5,480	2,950	3,360	5,040	-	2,800	80	4,120	1,050	650
Minnesota	15,580	33,120	10,080	57,120	1,600	51,800	980	97,120	1,960	63,340
Nebraska	7,720	-	-	660	1,870	1,050	1,850	2,450	450	2,200
New York	8,050	9,850	4,620	17,380	450	21,850	-	26,400	-	23,800
Ohio	29,070	1,530	23,310	3,790	12,010	8,690	7,110	13,790	1,960	7,840
Oregon	-	-	-	3,300	-	1,500	-	5,800	1,900	7,600
Pennsylvania	7,000	-	5,400	1,350	4,760	7,140	3,270	9,800	2,520	7,980
Tennessee	3,600	-	-	-	-	-	-	-	-	-
Utah	-	-	-	100	-	550	-	2,000	-	4,900
Virginia	-	-	320	2,400	410	90	180	420	-	500
Washington	-	-	-	2,880	-	3,900	1,810	11,090	670	8,930
Wisconsin	11,810	2,090	15,120	2,140	4,930	27,970	4,230	101,470	2,190	63,340
Other States	2,390	1,770	4,790	2,140	5,180	3,210	4,480	4,290	4,690	4,110
Total	292,590	73,900	254,060	164,970	130,140	204,430	109,080	423,530	70,320	287,810

Table 5.1   Acreage of Sweet Corn for Processing by Type.   *Source*: U.S.D.A. *Commercial Vegetables*, 1953, 67-71.

developed in the West were also used in Maine, New Hampshire and Vermont.[20]   This adoption of Idaho seed by Northern New England canners came after many other regions of the United States were using western grown seed. Wallace points out that as early as 1928:

> Between 70 and 80 percent of the hybrid sweet corn seed was grown in the Snake River Valley, near Caldwell and Boise, Idaho...
> The total acreage in Idaho was 7,000 to 8,000 acres annually... around 34 percent was used for canning factories... The inbred strains that made up the hybrid sweet corn were nearly all developed at the Iowa, Illinois, Connecticut, New York, Indiana, and Maine experiment stations.[21]

Maine also encouraged the use of improved varieties and better cropping practices by establishing raw sweet corn inspection and grading programs at canning factories. This was a volunteer operation, but processors and growers both supported the concept. In 1934 thirteen factories set up official grading programs of incoming corn. For 1935 it was twenty-three and 1936 had thirty-three shops grading. The number fell back to twenty-three in 1937, probably an indication of depression period price shifts and spot cannery closures.[22] The industry had improved its raw quality standards with both farmers and canners pushing for a high value end product.

Agricultural Innovations

In addition to improvements in canning procedure and sweet corn varieties, field cultivation and harvesting also changed. From 1931 to 1968 the tractor spread to nearly all farms. A study by Schrumpf and Pullen, *Costs and Returns in Sweet Corn Production: Central Maine 1955,* discovered that, of the seventy-three farmers in the sample, "tractors were used on sweet corn on 99 percent of the farms and trucks on 66 percent. Only seven percent used horses."[23] Both tractors and horses were used by some farmers. More efficient machinery came into use during these years. Plows, harrows, and planters improved while other pieces of equipment were introduced. Following the Second World War mechanical sweet corn harvesting increased. In the 20's and 30's a corn picker had been developed to handle field corn, but it could not be used to harvest tender sweet corn. Once a mechanical picker had been perfected that did not bruise the prime sweet corn kernels too much, hand picking began to decline. This innovation meant a reduction in labor force and an increase in harvest speed. Any increase in corn damage as a result of mechanical picking was probably more than offset by labor savings and speed. The changover did carry some risk. Damage and missed ears resulted in lower yield of high quality corn than hand picking in the Midwest for the 1954 and 55 seasons.[24] The small fields of New England were not so suitable to mechanical pickers as the big flatlands of the Midwest. Much valuable harvesting time had to be used in moving equipment from small field to small field, while in Indiana or Illinois the picker just kept picking. With the trend toward corn varieties that brought entire fields to uniform maturity at the same time (in some cases, many fields would mature all at once), mechanical pickers could keep up with the corn crop. But, much of it went into lower grades.[25] Fertilizers and chemicals came into increased use. In 1955 seventy-two of seventy-three sample farms in Central Maine used commercial fertilizer of some type in sweet corn production.[26] The increased usage of sprays as a means of controlling weeds and insects resulted in further reduction in the field workforce.

Although labor and time saving developments took place during the years following the 1930's, farms often lost money on sweet corn. Schrumpf and Pullen reveal that for 1955 the:

> ...cost of producing sweet corn on the 73 farms averaged $102.56 an acre and $32.06 a ton. Returns including the value of ears and the farmers' estimate of the value of the rest of the corn for feed and green manure averaged $99.49 an acre. This figures to an average net loss of $3.07 an acre.[27]

Labor was the largest cost, with fertilizer and lime rating a close second (Figure 5.8). Costs varied greatly, depending upon individual cultural practices, local physical conditions and size of operation. Increasing acreage per farm was a possible key to the reduction of costs. In general, the greater the acreage per farm, the lower the production costs per acre (Table 5.2). This variation in production costs is reflected in net returns for sweet corn on the farms (Table 5.3). Despite the many innovations, labor expenses continued to be the largest single cost. In 1955 the two most costly operations were picking the crop and hauling manure (Table 5.4). Plowing, hauling the raw corn to the cannery, hand hoeing, cultivating, planting and picking stones were also significant factors in the total cost of the crop. The last of these expenses is unique to the New England sweet corn producing

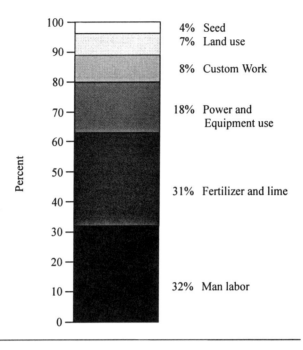

Figure 5.8   Cost Items in Producing Sweet Corn for Processing in Central Maine. *Source:* Adapted from Schrumph and Pullen, 1955, p.10.

area, because the production areas of the West and Midwest have few stones with which to contend. By 1955 the majority of the Northern New England sweet corn growers could not produce the crop at a profit. Because the processors controlled the market price, the only way the farmer influenced his gain or loss was by controlling production costs. Most could not keep their costs low enough to get a decent return, although in years of excessively high market prices a large portion of the growers acquired a sizeable net gain. Because years with low market prices were more frequent than years with high prices, an increasing number of growers stopped production as they discovered they were losing money. For the most part, larger growers were able to maintain production longer than small operators.

Item	1-3	4-6	7+	All Farms
Number of farms	35	20	18	73
Acres of sweet corn per farm	2.2	4.9	13.5	5.7
Yield per acre (pounds)	6,192	5,814	6,701	6,398
Costs per acre (dollars)				
Seed	4.50	4.06	3.94	4.07
Fertilizer and lime	26.96	28.27	34.86	31.83
Spray material	.36	.42	.89	.69
Man labor	48.27	44.66	22.48	32.52
Tractive power	18.92	16.02	9.62	12.86
Equipment	8.18	5.75	5.04	5.79
Land use	6.07	6.49	7.21	6.83
Custom work	4.00	5.24	10.36	7.97
All farms	117.28	110.91	94.40	102.56
Costs per ton (dollars)				
Seed	1.46	1.40	1.18	1.28
Fertilizer and lime	8.75	9.72	10.41	9.95
Spray material	.12	.15	.27	.21
Man labor	15.66	15.35	6.71	10.71
Tractive power	6.14	5.51	2.87	4.02
Equipment	2.65	1.97	1.50	1.81
Land use	1.96	2.23	2.15	2.13
Custom work	1.30	1.80	3.09	2.49
All farms	38.04	38.13	28.18	32.06
Per cent of total cost				
Seed	3.8	3.7	4.2	4.0
Fertilizer and lime	23.0	25.5	36.9	31.0
Spray material	0.3	0.4	1.0	0.7
Man labor	41.2	40.3	23.8	31.8
Tractive power	16.1	14.1	10.2	12.5
Equipment	7.0	5.2	5.3	5.6
Land use	5.2	5.8	7.6	6.6
Custom work	3.4	4.7	11.0	7.8
All farms	100.00	100.00	100.00	100.00

Table 5.2   Costs in Producing Sweet Corn for Processing on Different Acreages in Central Maine. *Source:* Schrumph and Pullen, 1955, p. 11.

Item	1-3	4-6	7+	All Farms
Returns per acre (in dollars)				
Ears	66.67	72.35	72.48	71.37
Stalks, etc.[a]	26.87	28.55	28.36	28.12
Total returns	93.54	100.90	100.84	99.49
Total costs	117.28	110.91	94.40	102.56
Net gain (or loss)	-23.74	-10.01	6.44	-3.07

[a] Cobs, husks and stalks actually used on the farm either as feed or green manure are credited to this item. Its addition to the value of the farmers' own corn by-products used on the farm, one-fourth of the farmers representing one-fifth of the sweet corn acreage used factory by-products which, if pro-rated on all farms, would have added an estimated $8.11 an acre to the average by-product value.

Table 5.3   Returns and Net Gain in Producing Sweet Corn for Processing in Central Maine, 1955. *Source:* Schrumph and Pullen, 1955, p. 12.

	HOURS PER ACRE			COST PER ACRE (dollars)			
Operation[a]	Acreage	Man	Power	Man	Power	Equipment	Total Cost
Hauling manure	67.1	8.0	6.0	$7.71	$4.19	$1.75	$13.65
Liming	44.7	1.1	0.8	1.08	0.62	0.18	1.88
Plowing	97.7	2.8	2.5	2.76	1.87	1.48	6.11
Disking (all)		1.5	1.5	1.52	1.14	0.68	3.34
Over once	100.0	0.7	0.7	0.71	0.53	0.32	1.56
Harrowing (all)		1.1	1.1	1.14	0.76	0.35	2.25
Over once	100.0	0.6	0.6	0.62	0.42	0.19	1.23
Picking stones	61.4	2.6	1.4	2.49	1.12	0.07	3.68
Planting	90.3	2.2	1.4	2.14	1.22	1.08	4.44
Weed spraying	22.8	0.8	0.6	0.71	0.42	0.23	1.36
Cultivating (all)		2.3	2.3	2.34	1.62	0.86	4.82
Over once	94.5	0.8	0.8	0.82	0.56	0.30	1.68
Side dressing	24.3	1.0	1.0	1.08	0.87	0.28	2.23
Hand hoeing	14.9	4.5	-	4.84	-	-	4.84
Hand picking	64.5	16.0	-	14.80	-	-	14.80
Hauling to factory	64.1	3.4	19.7[b]	3.47	2.05	-	5.52

[a] Times of disking averaged slightly more and times of harrowing slightly less than twice over. In planting, horses were used on 9.7 percent and in cultivation on 5.5 percent of the acreage. Tractor cultivation was performed an average of 2.8 times. In picking, 35.5 percent of acreage was custom machine work and the common charge was $15.00 an acre. In hauling to the factory 35.9 percent of the acreage was custom hauled.

[b] Truck miles

Table 5.4   Time and Cost Per Acre of the Operations in Growing Sweet Corn for Processing in Central Maine, 1955. *Source*: Schrumpf and Pullen, 1955, p. 16.

Farmers

The 1930's were a time of downward market pressure for agricultural products as the national economy struggled. Farmers entered this decade with great optimism but were soon battered and worn from financial stress. In 1929 high prices and excellent growing conditions had produced nice profits. By 1932 markets for most items were soft and nearly everything cost more to produce than it could be sold for. The Maine Farm Index had fallen to thirty-seven percent below the pre-World War One level, while the wholesale price index had dropped only five percent.[28] Despite hard times on farms, conditions were as bad or worse in urban places where workers lost jobs and all means of support.[29] Farmers could grow some vegetables, milk a cow, keep a few hens, cut wood for their heat and cling to the hope that next year would bring better prices. Some of the urban unemployed returned to family farms during the mid-1930's and helped keep agriculture going. Although tractors were part of the agrarian sector, most farms were partly dependent on draft animals and hand labor was still common in fields. Farms were a mix of commercial and subsistence with both being important in preventing rural communities from disappearing.[30]

Sweet corn was viewed as a possible money maker if prices went up a little. Fewer farmers would take a risk as their capital was depleted and canneries closed. Percent of farms reporting sweet corn as a crop in 1939 dropped to only five percent in the three states (Figure 4.2). The sweet corn grower felt fortunate if a local shop stayed open; when canning was done, companies often cut out some product lines. The Pittsfield, New Hampshire, B & M shop did not contract for beans in 1936 and this was"...regretted by many of the farmers."[31]

World War Two was beginning to be felt on the farm by 1940 as high demand for foodstuff preceeded the United States entry into combat. That same Pittsfield cannery that eliminated beans in '36 had a bumper year in 1941. Donald H. Farnham, superintendent, reported the total output that year was 1,336,037 cans of corn or nearly three times as much as in 1940."[32]

Prices finally went up and agriculture yielded profits. Farmers responded with increased production as the war progressed. By 1944 acreage was up to eighty-five percent of its 1929 highwater mark. Percent of farmers growing sweet corn remained at only about half the 29 level (Figure 4.2). Output per farm was up as a result of mechanical equipment and farmers tended to specialize more as the last of low commodity prices passed with the Depression. The early war years produced profits and optimism that resulted in farm investments. My family acquired its first tractor in 1943, a Ford with a full line of implements. By 1950 an observer was more likely to see a tractor working in a field than a pair of horses. The Frederic operation held onto its team, Dick and Pete, until 1957 because of winter lumbering needs. However, they did little farm work after 1950. With me as teamster, an occasional hayraking session for exercise was about the extent of their summer activity. Frederics were planting ten to twelve acres of corn for the cannery and an acre or two of beans. My 4-H project for the mid-50's was one-half acre of sweet corn. It seemed like a lot more at hoeing time!

The war had transformed the marketplace and agriculture and changes continued to manifest themselves into the 1960's. Farms became more specialized as milk, potatoes, eggs and broilers came to dominate agriculture in the area.[33] Choices had to be made; regulations forcing dairymen to shift from cans to bulk tanks required farmers to purchase new milk equipment to stay in production. Milk prices were more stable than those of sweet corn, making dairy a safer bet.

By 1954, percent of farmers reporting sweet corn had dropped to its lowest level since 1909 and acreage was well below that of 09'. Adoption of mechanical pickers and investment in trucks to haul corn to the more distant canneries, as the local one had closed, pushed up costs to such a level that most small and mid-sized growers stopped planting corn. Hand harvesting continued on small acreages and producers close to an operating shop could transport raw corn by tractor and wagon. The Frederic cornfields were a quarter mile from the factory and I spent much time during the 50's hauling corn in and waste for cattle feed out with that Ford tractor purchased in 1943. Some farmers invested in mechanical pickers for their own harvest and for custom work for other growers. This was risky business because return on the investment depended on the cannery staying in production. Farmer Milton Harris of New Sharon, Maine, with a partner, purchased a picker in the 1950's and harvested sweet corn on a number of local farms. His operation was located about midway between the New Sharon and Starks canneries (five miles to either). When the New Sharon shop burned in 1960 he lost much of his picking business and after the closure of the Starks factory in 1963 there was little demand for the machine.[34]

To ensure raw corn supplies, some canning companies expanded their own crop raising on purchased or leased land. They were better able to invested in farm equipment (tractor, plows, planters, pickers, etc.) than farmers. A growing season crew would be hired to care for this aspect of the enterprise. Monmouth Canning Company planned to plant seventy-four percent (993 of 1,350) of its required 1964 acreage for the Freedom, Maine, shop.[35] This land was scattered among Canton, Starks and Freedom (Canton and Starks factories had stopped canning) thus, trucking of fifty to sixty miles between field and factory was required. At the end only a handful of farms were growing sweet corn so that canner and farmer were often the same. Vertical integration, which was part of the changing nature of American agriculture, engulfed sweet corn canning in Maine, New Hampshire and Vermont.

Labor

Corn factory crews were more mature during the Depression and post-depression years (Figure 5.9). Mechanization, enforcement of school and child labor laws and high unemployment among adults pushed most underage employees out of the work force. A job at the shop was so coveted during the dark 1930's that almost any wage would attract applicants. In 1932 Edward Baker canned corn for $.35 per hour at the H .C. Baxter and Brothers factory in Essex Junction, Vermont. He left the cannery job to take one with Green Mountain Power Company which paid $20.70 per week, seven night shifts.[36] This was not a great jump in income. To make $20.70 at Baxter's would require 59.14 hours at $.35 each. Seven, eight hour shifts would total 56 hours at the power plant to earn the $20.70. However, the Green Mountain job was year-round, clean and stable. Individuals that couldn't find regular employment remained with the corn shops; as the economy weakened they were glad to have a job. When federal minimum wage standards were adopted in 1938 ($.25 per hour), canneries appear to have set their pay scale accordingly.[37] With the onset of wartime demands for both food and labor, corn shops were confronted with a labor shortage. Children were recruited to fill some of the gap. High school students were often given permission to work and even those under age 16 could be hired with special permits. These workers would often take over in the evening after the adults were tired.[38] When there were big backlogs

Figure 5.9   Corn Shop Crew,   Starks, Maine, 1936. *Source:* Gladys Lovell.

of unprocessed vegetables, the cannery owner would ask the local high school to excuse students from class to process the kernels.[39] In 1943 church services in Starks, Maine, were suspended during corn shop season to free workers for production.[40] Even God took a back pew!.

As the war wore on, labor shortfalls became an even greater problem and arrangements were made to tap the large German prisoners of war (POW) population. Several major prison camps had been established in Maine and New Hampshire to supply wood cutters for the forest industry. During the spring, summer and fall, some POW's were assigned to agricultural work and potato farmers in Aroostook County, Maine, took extensive advantage of this labor pool.[41] Canneries brought in Germans from a variety of camps. In some cases, POW's were transferred to housing closer to job locations. Bangor and Augusta in Maine, provided such facilities. The men were bussed or trucked under guard daily to the corn shops.[42] In some cases prisoners were boarded locally in homes.[43] Shops using POW's were in Hartland, New Sharon, Starks, Farmington (Franklin Farms), Albion and Corinna in Maine, and Pittsfield, New Hampshire, and Randolph, Vermont.[44]

Teenagers Linwood Currier and Jeanetta Stevens, recall POW's arriving by bus at the canneries in New Sharon and Farmington.[45] Sayward Hackett remembers them at Starks, where he was raking corn in the sheds. The guards with carbines seem to have impressed him as much as the Germans.[46] Mary Croswell encountered one of the POW's who spoke some English and responded, when asked if he was married, "My wife is married, but I'm not!"[47] Richard Gould, son of Franklin Farms cannery owner, reports that the company was satisfied with their work.[48]

With the end of the war and repatriation of POW's by late 1946, the composition of corn shop labor changed again. Returning G.I.'s were available to work and they filled many of the assignments in the canning business. There were growing opportunities for year round milltown and service sector jobs. The G.I. Bill provided fiscal support to attend college. Fewer men were interested in patching together a series of part-time and seasonal jobs.

When the shop was operating, production continued until all the vegetables that had been brought in were in cans. There were few scheduled breaks; thus, from the worker's perspective, the occasional unexpected one was usually welcome. A memorable stoppage occurred one weekend at the Starks factory. The cannery had a shutdown because of mechanical problems. There happened to be a dance at the Town Hall and Mr. Edwards, plant superintendent, told the women they could go to the dance, and he would send someone to get them when repairs had been completed. Many of them got the corn juice off as best they could and went to the dance for a few hours before being called back to work.[49] A good song writer might have been able to make a hit with "Swing Your Corn Shop Girl Tonight!" Considering working conditions, management was often flexible in giving people a chance to enjoy a breakdown. Morale needed to be maintained.

Some plant owners, employed in occupations unrelated to the canneries, required special permission from their employers to run their seasonal canning business. Richard Gould, who also taught at the local high school, had an agreement with the School Committee that allowed him to be absent from his classroom until the year's corn and beans were packed. This policy continued into the 1960's.[50]

Women were also driven by a new agenda. They discovered full-time year round employment in a wide variety of positions: mills, store clerks, professions etc. and found the six-week rat-race of the canning season did not fit into their life styles any more. The post-war baby boom also committed some women to domestic obligations.

These trends continued until the end of the sweet corn industry in the area. Poor weather complicated growing and harvesting and in those bad seasons little corn came into the shops. Some seasons the anticipated run of four to six weeks would turn out to be only seven or eight days.[51] Disappointment would be felt throughout the community. Firms that diversified and extended their season by adding products that had the potential to provide enough income from a single job to support their employees did tend to survive. Burnham & Morrill was able to accomplish this at their South Paris, Maine, cannery by processing more kinds of vegetables and brownbread.[52] Roy Demeritt, who owned factories in Randolph and Waterbury, Vermont, solved the seasonal labor issue by keeping a crew occupied in his clothespin manufacturing business for most of the year and shifting them to canning when the crops were ready for packing.[53]

A few efforts were made to find other labor sources. In the mid-1940's Blacks were employed in Franklin County, Maine, canneries.[54] In the 50's, the Jewett factory in Norridgewock, Maine, used county prisoners delivered in the morning and picked up at night by the Sheriff.[55] Field help was also brought in from Canada, Jamaica, and the South. Mechanical pickers soon replaced much of the field crew. With each passing year, labor supply became a greater problem, so that by the mid-1960's, the crews were composed of a few old timers who did not need year round employment, housewives that were interested in a little extra money in the fall, college kids about to return to classes, high school students for late afternoon and weekends, and a variety of individuals who had trouble holding regular jobs.[56]

Loss of the Industry to Other Areas

The improvement in quality and increased quantity of Western and Midwestern grown sweet corn was a constant concern in Northern New England. Murphy points out that, "For many years Maine sweet corn producers held considerable advantage over other producing areas, in yield per acre and quality. This advantage began to decrease in the late 1930's. Today [1954] it is negligible..."[57] By 1965 Idaho, Oregon, and Washington had yields significantly greater than Maine. Additionally, New York, Pennsylvania, Illinois, Minnesota, Delaware, and Maryland

received higher prices than Maine (Tables 4.7 and 4.8). The primary
cause for higher yielding and better quality sweet corn in other areas
was the hybrid strains. In a 1949 paper, R. M. Bailey states:

> The widespread development and acceptance of sweet corn hybrids has
> not been confined entirely to Maine's advantage. This state gained its
> early enviable reputation for high quality sweet corn in a large measure
> because of climatic advantage. The cool temperature with normally ample
> rainfall provides natural conditions that favor the development of a high
> quality raw product that is held at the optimum conditions for a
> comparatively long period at harvest time. In Maine the use of the more
> uniform maturing hybrids has helped to make a good canned product
> better, but under Midwest conditions, hybrids, uniform fields, proper
> timing of harvest, and faster handling of the raw product have all been
> important factors in improvement, particularly in Midwestern areas.
> Therefore, if we are to maintain our position in the sweet corn canning
> industry, we must exercise extreme care all along the line of production
> and processing to meeting the competition of other areas and preserve
> Maine's reputation for high quality canned corn.[58]

The loss of these advantages placed Maine, New Hampshire and
Vermont corn canners and growers in a marginal position.
     In 1953 it was discovered that processing costs were somewhat
higher for Northern New England canners than for other areas. Pullen
points out:

> A dozen No. 303 cans of cream-style corn costs the Maine canner $1.42
> in the warehouse ready for delivery, the New York canner $1.34 and the
> Midwest canner $1.30 (Table 5.5). Reasons for higher costs were
> indicated in part by the fact that direct labor costs were greater in Maine
> by six cents a dozen cans over the Midwest, and two cents over New
> York. Since wage rates were about the same, higher labor costs in Maine
> were due primarily to lower operating efficiency. Furthermore, it was
> revealed that the volume of output per plant in New York and the
> Midwest was three to four times greater than in Maine (Table 5.6). Small
> volume per plant, higher labor and raw product costs combine to put the
> Maine canner in an unfavorable cost position.[59]

The competitive position for the Maine and Vermont canner was
even more unfavorable for whole kernel style sweet corn. Economy of

	Cream-style corn			Whole-kernel corn		
	Maine-Vermont	New York	Mid-west[a]	Maine-Vermont	New York	Mid-west[a]
Raw Product at Plant	$0.40	$0.38	$0.32	$0.52	$0.37	$0.37
Direct Labor	0.17	0.15	0.11	0.20	0.13	0.12
Other Costs	0.85	0.81	0.87	0.83	0.76	0.86
Total Cost (Ready For Delivery)	$1.42	$1.34	$1.30	$1.55	$1.26	$1.35

[a] Minnesota and Wisconsin

Table 5.5 Comparison of Costs in Processing Canned Sweet Corn, Maine-Vermont, New York, and Midwest, 1953 Pack. *Source:* Pullen, 1956, p. 15.

	Cream-style corn			Whole-kernel corn		
	Maine-Vermont	New York	Mid-west[a]	Maine-Vermont	New York	Mid-west[a]
Average number of cases of #303 cans by plant	42,744	134,540	159,937	23,328	107,714	159,937
Average number of cases of #303 cans of cut corn per ton	36.9	36.17	36.50	28.91	33.96	31.00

[a] Minnesota and Wisconsin

Table 5.6 Comparison of Sweet Corn Production by Plants, Maine-Vermont, New York, and Midwest, 1953 Pack. *Source:* Pullen, 1956, p. 15.

scale was clearly to the Midwest's advantage. In 1953 the average cannery in Illinois processed corn from 4,186 acres.[60] The average for thirteen plants in Wisconsin for 1955 was 1,476.[61] For a Northern New England shop at that time, the average was about 500-600 acres. Canneries in the West and Midwest held labor cost down while ensuring a stable supply by employing large numbers of migrant workers. The Joan of Arc and Stokely-Van Camp Companies operated large processing plants in Hoopeston, Illinois, supported by 1,200 field and cannery migrants during the 1971 season. A few years earlier the number of such workers approached 3,000. Working and living conditions left much to be desired.[62] Squalid migrant camps were a far cry from the New England village, but they were part of the sweet corn canning movement to the West. In a study of seven selected Middle Atlantic and Midwestern corn canning plants, Collins and Savage found that processors could make significant economic gains by increasing their yearly volume, daily volume, case yields per ton of raw product and uniformity of raw product flow to the plant.[63] An unpublished paper by John Gault indicated that the cost differences between Northern New England canners and those of other areas increased rather than decreased during the 1950's. By 1958, the average New England cost was nine cents per dozen cans higher than New York, and fifteen cents per dozen greater than Wisconsin-Minnesota costs.[64]

Although the Maine, New Hampshire and Vermont canners were handicapped by greater production costs, nearness to northeastern markets helped to offset this disadvantage to a certain extent. Southern New England served as the major market area for the region's corn canners, with Massachusetts accounting for thirty-two percent of the consumption (Figure 5.10). Thirty-two percent went to markets outside of New England, while only eighteen percent remained in the three upper New England states. This market pattern may be attributed, in part, to the shipping advantage enjoyed by Northern New England corn canners (Table 5.7). In 1954, Farmington, Maine, shippers held an advantage over other major areas transporting to the Boston market. Because truck rates were lower, railroads played a secondary role. As distance increased from Farmington, rail became more significant. The Farmington shippers had lower costs to New York City markets than Midwest canners, but greater than Middle Atlantic processors. Most of the Northern New England canned corn moved through chain stores and wholesalers (Figure 5.11). Only four percent moved directly from

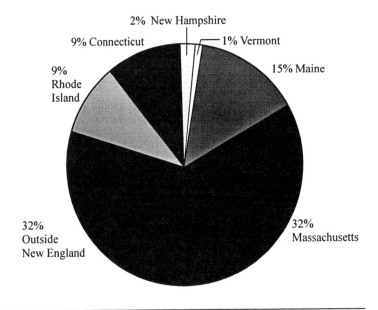

2% New Hampshire
9% Connecticut
1% Vermont
9% Rhode Island
15% Maine
32% Outside New England
32% Massachusetts

Figure 5.10   Market Area for Northern New England Canned Sweet Corn, 1953. *Source:* Pullen, 1956, p. 20.

processors to retailer or other buyers. For the most part, corn packed in the area was sold with buyer label. Seventy-two percent of the corn sold to wholesalers was under buyer label, while ninety-six percent of chain store sales was under this type of label (Table 5.8). Only seventeen percent of the corn to other sources had buyers' labels, while thirty-two percent had the sellers' label. These data indicate that the canners' label was more likely to find its way into the small retail store that purchased directly from the processor than into the large-scale chain stores, such as First National or Kroger. When buyer labels are used the consumer has a tendency to associate the quality of the product with the store that handled the goods rather than the processor who may remain unknown. In his study Pullen points out:

> The fact that more than forty brand names are used for Maine sweet corn does not permit effective merchandising and development of consumer preference for Maine corn. A consumer is virtually bewildered when confronted with this battery of brand names.[65]

Shipping Point	Actual Rate Per One Hundred Pounds in Cents		Freight Advantage in Shipping From Farmington, Maine, per dozen #303 cans in cents
	To Boston		To Boston
	Cost	Cost Difference	
Farmington, Maine[a]	.41		
Baltimore, Maryland	.53	.12	1.5
Hanover, Pennsylvania	.53	.12	1.5
Indianapolis, Indiana	.81	.40	5.1
La Suer, Minnesotta	1.17	.76	9.6
Madison, Wisconsin	.89	.48	6.1
Rochester, New York[a]	.52	.11	1.4
Springfield, Illinois	.91	.50	6.3
	To New York City		To New York City
	Cost	Cost Difference	
Farmington, Maine[a]	.61		
Baltimore, Maryland	.32	-.29	- 3.7
Hanover, Pennsylvania	.32	-.29	- 3.7
Indianapolis, Indiana	.77	.16	2.0
La Suer, Minnesotta	1.11	.50	6.3
Madison, Wisconsin	.87	.26	3.3
Rochester, New York[a]	.44	-.17	- 2.2
Springfield, Illinois	.89	.28	3.5

[a] Represents shipment by truck since at lower cost.

Table 5.7   Costs of Shipping Canned Sweet Corn From Farmington, Maine, Compared to Costs From Other Shipping Points to Boston and New York City Markets, 1954. *Source:* Pullen, 1955, p. 14.

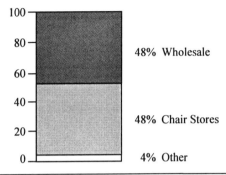

Figure 5.11   Receivers of Sweet Corn Packed by Maine Canners, 1953. *Source:* Pullen, 1955, p. 22).

| | Proportion of Sales To Each Receiver | | |
	Wholesaler	Chain Store	Other
Buyer	72	96	17
Seller	24	3	32
No Label	4	1	51
Total	100	100	100

Table 5.8   Types of Labels on Maine Canned Sweet Corn,1953.*Source:* Pullen, 1955, p.22.

Of six sample urban markets (Portland, Maine; Cincinnati, Ohio; St. Paul, Minnesota; Washington, D.C.; Milwaukee, Wisconsin; and Seattle, Washington), only the Portland consumers rated a Maine canned sweet corn among their first four preferences. Burnham & Morrill and H. C. Baxter and Brother were both popular processors, although they ranked behind the First National brand name FINAST.[66] As it became more and more evident that Northern New England corn canners were not making a profit, additional shops closed. The great influx of canned corn from the West more than offset the decreased production of Maine, New Hampshire and Vermont. The value of the 1965 Maine sweet corn crop for processing was only $144,000 while eight other states had over $1,000,000 worth of sweet corn for processing and the national value was $36,159,000 (Table 4.5).

The location quotient is used to demonstrate the geographical redistribution of sweet corn processing. "Location quotient measures the degree to which a region has more or less than its share of an industry."[67] The location quotient is determined by (1) Computing the state's value of all vegetables for processing as a percentage of the national total, (2) Computing the state's share of the value of sweet corn for processing as a percentage of the national value of sweet corn for processing, and (3) Comparing the state's value of sweet corn percentage with the state's value of vegetables for processing percentage. In the following formula **A** = Value of all vegetables for processing by state, **B** = Value of all vegetables for processing within the United States, **C** = Percentage of the national value of all vegetables for processing by state, **D** = Value of sweet corn processing by state, **E** = Value of sweet corn for processing within the United States, and **F** = Percentage of the national value of sweet corn for processing by state.

$$\frac{D/E}{A/B} = \frac{F}{C} = \text{Location Quotient}$$

For example, in 1960 the value of all Maine vegetables grown for processing was $1,642,000 compared to the national value of $287,161,000 (Appendix B). Maine's sweet corn for processing had a value of $339,000 while the national had $26,768,000 worth of the crop for processing (Table 4.5). The 1960 location quotient for the state is:

$$\frac{339,000 \ / \ 26,768,000}{1,642,000 \ / \ 287,161,000} = \frac{.0126}{.0057} = 2.210$$

A location quotient of 1.0 means that a state has neither more nor less of the national value of sweet corn for processing than its overall value of vegetables for processing would suggest. A quotient over 1.0 indicates a high concentration in that state, relative to all vegetable processing. A quotient of less than 1.0 suggests that the sweet corn processing industry is less developed in that state than vegetable processing in general.

The relative change in the importance of the sweet corn canning industry for the leading corn processing states indicates a decline in Northern New England and a rise in the Midwest and West between

1930 and 1965 (Table 5.9). In 1930 Maine, New Hampshire, and Vermont had the three highest location quotients while the Midwestern states of Illinois, Minnesota, Iowa, and Nebraska all had quotients greater than 4.0. The importance of Maine's sweet corn processing steadily decreased. By 1965 the state's location quotient was only .95. New Hampshire and Vermont also had declining location quotients and by 1960 production was so low that the United States Department of Agriculture stopped publishing values of sweet corn for processing in those states. During the thirty-five years between 1930 and 1965, many Midwestern and Western states found sweet corn processing a growing part of their vegetable industry. Wisconsin's location quotient increased from .29 in 1930 to 2.42 in 1965; Minnesota rose from 4.53 to 5.27. Data for 1930 are not available, but beginning with 1940 it is evident that a rapid development took place in the Northwest; Idaho increased

	1930	1940	1950	1960	1965
Maine	6.64	5.25	2.90	2.21	.95
New Hampshire	8.00	13.00	3.66	NA	NA
Vermont	9.00	7.80	7.66	NA	NA
Delaware	.47	.33	.61	.59	.40
Idaho	NA	3.60	4.63	4.48	4.70
Illinois	4.75	3.46	3.71	3.11	3.19
Indiana	.82	.88	.83	NA	NA
Iowa	5.82	4.56	5.50	2.25	2.29
Maryland	.72	1.30	1.17	2.19	1.88
Michigan	.16	.15	.06	NA	NA
Minnesota	4.53	5.58	5.29	5.00	5.27
Nebraska	6.00	5.36	3.66	NA	NA
New York	.69	.73	1.22	1.00	.94
Ohio	1.64	1.24	1.01	NA	NA
Oregon	NA	.35	.87	1.43	1.76
Pennsylvania	1.33	1.11	.81	.91	.77
Tennessee	1.00	NA	NA	NA	NA
Utah	NA	.20	1.27	NA	NA
Virginia	NA	.06	.07	NA	NA
Washington	NA	.85	.90	1.44	1.64
Wisconsin	.29	1.17	1.49	2.46	2.42
Other States	.03	.04	.08	.14	.06

Table 5.9   Location Quotient for Sweet Corn. *Source:* Computed by author. Raw data appear in Table 4.5 and Appendix B.

from 3.60 to 4.70 by 1965; Washington's quotient changed from .85 to 1.64 and Oregon's from .35 to 1.76. Maryland is the only other state to show an increase in the importance of sweet corn processing. Although location quotients decreased, the crop continued to play an important role in Illinois and Iowa.

Maine, New Hampshire, and Vermont companies adopted a variety of strategies to contend with emerging trends. Some canneries such as W. S. Wells in Wilton, Maine, dropped sweet corn by the early 50's and concentrated on niche markets including fiddleheads and dandelions with success.[68] Burnham & Morrill slowly shifted to other products. The company's advertisements in the *Maine Registrar* from 1920 to 1960 demonstrate change. A one-quarter page advertisement in 1920 promotes nine canned products all in the same font with sweet corn listed third. In 1940 the same format has demoted sweet corn to seventh among eleven items. In 1950 baked beans had bold block letter print with "also sea foods, vegetables, specialties" and in 1960 its half page is on baked beans.[69] B & M baked beans remain a canned product to this day. Monmouth Canning Company continued to play the corn card fairly high to the end, although it canned baked beans and blueberries as well as other vegetables. Until the early 1960's it was still considered a major player in food processing. The front cover of Maine's Department of Agriculture *Biennial Report for 1962-1964* doesn't suggest the end was so near (Figure 5.12). In the photograph, Chester Soule of the Monmouth Canning Company is overseeing the loading of a shipment of sweet corn in Portland aboard the nuclear ship SAVANNAH bound for Scandinavia.[70] If not the last, it's probably one of the last shipments of canned corn to leave the state by water. Isaac Winslow would undoubtedly have mixed feelings about the event. The SAVANNAH was a far different vessel than the tall masted whalers that transported much of his corn. Isaac Winslow could never have imagined a nuclear ship replacing the wooden sailing vessels, nor is it likely he anticipated the demise of his beloved corn industry.

In 1968 Northern New England's remaining corn shop processed its last cans of gold. Only ten years earlier, the area's corn canning businesses had been valued at $2.5 million.[71] The corn shop century ended.

Figure 5.12   Maine Corn for Scandinavia, 1962-1964. *Source:* Maine
Department of Agriculture.

Chapter 6

People and Corn Shops

Small rural communities where canneries were located during the "corn shop century," 1860's-1960's considered themselves blessed. Farmers, cannery owners and workers stood to profit. For the most part, the various interests worked together harmoniously. This chapter draws extensively from interviews with former growers, owners and workers as well as my half century of observing these places pass from canning gold to panning for other opportunities.

I am acquainted with many individuals that have been involved with the sweet corn canning business, especially in central Maine. To extend my reach to others familiar with the industry, in January, 2000, I placed an invitation in twenty-seven local newspapers in Maine, New Hampshire and Vermont asking former corn shop workers to contact me for a possible interview. Sixty-one responded by letter, phone, email or word-of-mouth. These individuals were added to the pool of acquaintances. From this list of one hundred, seventy-five were interviewed; farmers, shop owners, superintendents, and workers.

Farmers

Farms within corn hauling distance of a shop were able to produce a dependable cash crop in a region where other options were limited. The Mallory Farm in South Strong was one of the larger sweet corn producers in the Farmington, Maine, area during the early 1950's. Allan Wyman's father managed the property for an absentee owner. The farm included 150 acres of cropland, 3,500 to 4,000 taps for maple syrup and a large herd of cattle. About 75 acres of sweet corn were grown for the

Farmington B & M plant. Labor to pick corn was always a problem. Blacks were sometimes brought in to help with harvesting. After graduating from high school in 1961, Wyman accepted a mill job and had only one more brief contact with canning sweet corn when he took a two week vacation from his wood turning mill job to work at the Franklin Farms corn shop. He earned enough extra money to buy his first good shotgun but left the experience, thinking that not many normal people worked in canneries.[1]

Few farmers relied entirely on sweet corn for a large portion of income but significant numbers grew some acreage. With increased agricultural specialization and a narrowing profit margin for the crop, by the 1960's only about five percent of the farms in Northern New England were still producing the crop for canning. Of the few companies that remained in operation, several were growing most of their own crop. Occasionally a farmer, like Milton Harris of New Sharon, Maine, would expand sweet corn acreage and invest in new equipment to meet market opportunities.[2]

Raising and harvesting sweet corn was carefully timed to ensure that a top quality crop was delivered to the shop. Growers took the following factors into account when selecting sites for corn: soils; elevation and slope for cold air drainage; and distance from other corn fields to protect from unwanted pollination. Planting was spaced to accommodate the full canning season; thus, the cannery could be used to its maximum capacity for the entire processing season. After the seed was in the ground, it was a battle to protect the corn from weeds, bugs, blight, raccoons, bears, cattle that escaped from their pasture, and human thieves searching for a few ears in the middle of the night. Francis Fenton remembers that his father grew about two acres of corn for the Mercer, Maine, shop each year it operated and planted corn close to the house to make it easier to keep crows and wild animals away.[3] The author recalls many long, hot mid-summer days of hoeing sweet corn.

A story passed to me by my father, Glenn, before his death in 1984 recounts that farmers sometimes resorted to violence to defend their corn. Marcellus Frederic, my grandfather, watched over his crop like a hawk. A nearby farmer, James Greaton, had a reputation for poor fences. After Greaton's cattle had invaded grandfather's corn field several times, each followed by a stern warning to Mr. Greaton, real trouble began to brew. One evening, after sustaining another round of destruction, farmer Frederic paid a visit to farmer Greaton with the intention of putting a stop to the problem. As Frederic approached Greaton's barn, the offender appeared armed with a pitchfork and gave little indication of any willingness to be cooperative about keeping his cows in their pasture. A few sharp words led to a punch from Frederic that brought the discussion to closure. Soon the sheriff was in contact with Frederic and he was ordered to court where guilt was found resulting in a modest fine for the assault. Grandfather's response was, "If I had known that it wasn't going to cost me more than that, I would have hit him again!" Greaton improved his fences fairly quickly.

Usually the most thrilling part of the growing season was just before harvest when the raccoons started to attack the corn. Any backyard gardener knows these animals have an uncanny ability to get to the ears just two or three days before the grower wants to pick them, no matter when picking is planned. It was always exciting when my father would call in professional coon hunters with their dogs. What teenage kid wouldn't insist on tagging along? These situations would usually turn into all-night adventures of treeing and shooting the masked corn bandits. Working the flashlight and gun was a lot more fun than the monotonous hoe!

In addition to problems that farmers had some control over, weather was always a worry. Late and early frosts could wipe out a crop; whereas, dry or wet seasons reduced yield and quality. When the cannery's fieldman gave the word to pick, harvesting became top priority and the field crews were quickly assembled. Men, women and children who were not working at the corn shop could always find employment harvesting. Field workers for both weed control and picking were largely local; although, there were several efforts to use imported help. German POW's were on a few central Maine farms late in World War II and African Americans from the southern U.S. played a minor role in the Franklin County, Maine, area.[4] In both situations there appears to have been a significant cultural gap between the communities and workers from away.

I often found myself part of the field crew as well as hauling corn to the shop. During the peak of the canning season, trucks and tractors pulling wagons laden with corn would be lined up waiting to unload at the corn shop. Farmers were also hauling waste husks and cobs away from the shop for cattle feed. When I wasn't going from field to factory, I was going from factory to silo. These were long days full of interaction with both pickers in the field and cannery workers while waiting to unload corn or to load waste. In the end, farmers hoped that their corn check would be greater than their production costs. Some considered the livestock feed value of the waste a major benefit of growing corn for the factory. Phil Andrews, a retired dairy farmer who milked 300 cows and raised 100 acres of sweet corn on his Fryeburg, Maine, farm during the 1950's to the 60's, reported:

> "From a farmers view corn shops were a great thing. But it was better when they closed. The corn shop crew made more pay than the farmers did growing corn. The cattle feed from the shop was the best part of growing corn. After the shops closed and I started raising cattle corn, I found it was much better than the sweet corn waste. Getting a picking crew was always a problem. There would be 3 or 4 pickers one day and maybe the next I could get 6 or 7 and then the next might be 3 or 4 again. The corn had to be picked when it was ready to go to the factory. It was awful nerve racking. I was glad to see mechanical pickers which came in about 10 years before the shops closed. Burnham & Morrill had two mechanical harvesters. That was much more enjoyable for the farmers." [5]

Farmers realized that sweet corn production was a way of spreading their risk with two possible returns, the corn check and waste for feed. In a region of few cash crops and high feed costs, corn for canning was an attractive choice for many small farm operations. Increased agricultural specialization, other competitive feed options such as lower cost grain from the west, development of short growing season cattle corn varieties, and narrowing sweet corn profits contributed to the decline in numbers of growers. A decrease in farm numbers throughout the region also helped transform the relationship among farmers, canners and their towns.

Owners

Corn shop owners came from diverse backgrounds; social standing, education and wealth varied. Would-be governors, farmers and backyard tinkerers established and operated canneries. Some, like John Burnham and Charles Morrill of Portland, Maine, saw their investment grow into major food processing firms with numerous factories canning corn and other produce. Others, such as Walter S. Wells of North Anson, Maine (later of Wilton, Maine), established a successful multi-generational, family-owned business that continues to can specialty items but not corn. Owners were viewed as important members of both state and local communities. They or their agents were leaders who worked closely with farmers, workers and other business people in the rural towns of Northern New England.

Ephriam Jillson's recollection of his boyhood as a corn shop owner's son provides insight into community linkage to the cannery and financial success in the business. His grandfather, Ephraim B. Jillson had, in partnership with others, built a corn shop in Otisfield, Maine, which opened at the turn of the nineteenth-twentieth century. Jillson soon bought out the other backers and operated it as sole owner until his son, George, married. At that time he gave the corn shop to George and moved to nearby Oxford, Maine.

"I was born in 1916. My father (George) had a good education and was a lawyer in Boston, but liked the outdoors and was interested in returning to rural Otisfield. He married an Irish girl from South Boston and, when offered a chance to take over his father's (Ephriam B.) corn shop and farm, moved his family to Maine. The property included the shop and large farm. The house had 30 rooms and people boarded there on a regular basis. The corn canning business had been good and he knew how to manage it. Father used to make sure good seed was used and raised 16 acres of corn for that purpose. He would put ears on spurs (boards with nails driven through to impale the ears on for drying) and hang them in the attic. Farmers that grew corn for him would use his seed and he also provided fertilizer. He would check the farmers' fields during the summer, and, if they were not hoed right, he would send a crew to care for the corn. He had 6 or 8 men working all summer and was very fussy about how each field was doing. One man didn't have any legs and he used a short handled hoe for working the rows. He could hoe like the devil and would beat the other guys. When he got to the end of the row, he, like the rest of the men, would take a swig of cider. Then the jug would be moved over to the next row. Father always had plenty of hard cider and home brew for the haying crew and corn helpers. He was his own fieldman, and, when the sweet corn was ready, he told the farmer to pick it and bring it to the shop.

He hired a lot of help at the shop. Before husking machines came along he would sometimes hire whole families. When my grandfather started the shop all the cans were made by hand. He would go to Oxford Station to pick up tin. Later a sealer was installed, and ready made cans were used. Continental Can Company sold cans and rented out the sealer. The machine was not for sale. Canned corn was shipped in wooden boxes with stenciled labels to indicate shop of production. The pack was hauled to Oxford Station by horses or truck. My father always used spring water in his corn and didn't use corn starch. Most canners put some corn starch in their product. Father packed a solid pack. During the last of his canning, about two-thirds of his production went to S. S. Pierce, a top of the line market. I remember one evening in the fall of 1923 when I was seven years old and down at the corn shop with my father. We were waiting for the last retort when he lifted me up so I could put wood into the firebox; this resulted in the retort blowing out. That was the last one to blow at our shop. We went home and to bed. Father never got up; his appendix burst before morning and he was dead at 43.

He had done well since returning to Otisfield. Between the farm and corn shop father made $100,000 some years. Playing the stock market also helped him. One year, about 1921, we went to Florida for the winter. Departure was on a stormy Thanksgiving Day. We were having family dinner when my grandfather told us, since we were all packed and snow was coming down, it would be best to get going. We had an old Model T with side curtains and at about 2:00 in the afternoon we started out and reached Wells, Maine, a distance of about 65 miles by night. We stayed there with relatives, got up early the next morning and drove to Boston. At that point the car was loaded on a freighter and we took passage to Savannah, Georgia. Because of limited space, the top of the car had to be put down to load it. The trip was rough with mother and father getting seasick. We kids were fine. The family stayed in Savannah for a while until a house was found to rent in Daytona, Florida. While in Florida we met a young fellow who was involved with the Dole pineapple operation in Hawaii. He asked my father to join him as a company lawyer. Mother would have nothing to do with the idea. Father wanted to buy some property in Florida but mother wouldn't let him.

My young mother, with small children, realized she could not manage the farm and shop and soon after father's death, sold the farm. Shortly afterwards the farm buildings burned. Later she sold most of the corn shop equipment to grandfather's original partners, who now owned the Keene and True Canning Company. About 1930, a junk dealer stole the boiler out of the shop and did great damage to the building. Mother got mad about the loss and had the structure taken down. The lot is now overgrown with brush."[6]

The Monmouth Canning Company, a larger successful enterprise, spanned half-a-century and four Soule generations. Peter Soule, who was involved with the sale of the company in the 1960's recounts the owner's view of the world.

"The company had originated as a partnership between my great grandfather, Elwin Soule, and a Mr. Cuskely, who started a corn shop in Gorham, Maine, before 1900. They later moved their operation to Monmouth, Maine, named the company for the town and reduced the number of owners to one, Mr. Soule. By purchase of existent canneries or construction of new ones, the firm expanded to a half dozen shops with its focus on corn, squash, beans (string and baked), brownbread and blueberries. Company headquarters and the baked bean and brown bread operation were in Portland with the seasonal shops located in the Maine communities of Monmouth, Freedom, Liberty, Union, Starks and Canton. Seth, Elwin's son, took over as chief executive officer.

The Soule family lived in Cape Elizabeth, Maine, a suburb of Portland, and I recall going to work for the company in 1959 as a young man in my mid-twenties. I spent two years studying agricultural engineering at the University of Maine before going into the armed service. Following discharge, I continued to study food preservation technology in Boston, and my first assignment for the company was to supervise the Union plant which I did for two years. In 1961 I became roving manager and worked closely with my father, Chester, and uncle, Ralph on business decisions. There was a tradition of family members being close to the shops during canning season. In the 1930's and early 40's Ralph stayed in the company residence in Starks when packing was being done. In the 1950's a friend of my father, Charles Bailey, was brought into the company and eventually took over much of its management.

During the 1940's and 50's Monmouth Canning Company was one of the larger canning firms. However, there were too many negative things coming together to keep the business going. To ensure steady quality and quantity of the raw product, we took over more of the farming aspect of the business, although some farmers continued to grow until shop closure. At many of the plants the whole family would be employed and the canning season had a social as well as economic atmosphere. Near the end it was much less social. Mechanical harvesters did away with most of the hand pickers and it was increasingly difficult to find shop workers. Western competition was growing more intense in the canned corn markets. The old outdated small shops didn't warrant large investment to upgrade. There were some efforts to consolidate operations but they were not successful for corn. In 1963 we closed the Canton and Starks factories and tried to boost production at Freedom. We couldn't get enough corn close to the plant and had to truck it 40-50 miles.

Sometimes large loads would come into the yard with steam rolling from them, a sure sign that the ears were overheating and quality was down.

Environmental challenges from shop waste were an ongoing problem. Large amounts of materials were discharged into waterways and we were battling regulators. Some of the best wild ducks were raised on corn waste in the streams, but the Maine Department of Environmental Protection didn't see it that way! Government workplace rules were also becoming a threat.

In addition to production and regulation concerns, the company was confronted with the State Department of Transportation taking, by eminent domain, its Portland property. Compensation offered was not near building replacement costs and the firm would lose its year-round baked bean and brown-bread facility. The small seasonal shops could not support the operation. A. L Stewart Company had an extensive blueberry processing business in eastern Maine and expressed an interest in the remainder of our assets. String beans had been an excellent performer in the early 1960's. Stewart thought the berry and bean sectors would be solid additions to his company. We decided to sell to Stewart. I continued to work for the company as manager of their blueberry interest in the Union, Maine, area. Later Stewart sold to Allen's blueberry firm and I remained as their area supervisor until retirement at age 62. Canning was a good family business for three generations (great grandfather, grandfather and father) and was still doing well when I was first involved.[7]

From a local community perspective the Soules were welcome in the small towns where their company had shops. In Starks, Ralph Soule had a second interest as part owner of a skewer mill which provided employment for some of the corn shop crew when canning wasn't in production.[8] Wooden skewers were widely used in the meat business until the mid-1900's when plastic and other handling techniques resulted in a reduction in their demand. As a child, I remember my parents commenting from time to time that the Soules were in town. It was a noteworthy event. I recall a little childhood ditty sometimes heard on the schoolyard during the fall canning season: "Old Seth Soule is a merry old soul and a merry old soul is he!"

Employees

Canning company employees varied from people who were engaged in the operation year-round to individuals that might have a short career consisting of only a day or so. During 2000, I interviewed sixty-five former corn shop workers and a few owners and managers.

Superintendents

In some situations, owner and shop superintendents were the same, but most superintendents were hired on a salary basis and often remained for years. This position included all responsibilities for cannery management and field operations. Some families would hold these jobs for several generations and maintain a strong bond with the business. Edward Jones of Fryeburg, Maine, documents this pattern.

> "My family has been involved with corn canning since 1895. My great grandfather, who had the same name as myself, came from Wilton, Maine, to Conway, New Hampshire, in 1895 to run the corn shop there and in 1902 moved to North Fryeburg. In 1903 he bought the house next door to where we are and in 1918 he purchased this house. There were lots of shops around here: Fryeburg Harbor, West Fryeburg, North Fryeburg, East Fryeburg, Fryeburg Center and Conway just across the state line. When my great grandfather retired from Snowflake Canning Company, which had been purchased by Baxter Brothers, my father took over the shop and my great grandfather remained in charge of syrup mixing. My grandfather didn't have as much to do with the shops, although he was foreman at the Harbor cannery for a time. My father ran the Baxter plant in North Fryeburg. My great-grandmother managed a cookhouse for cannery workers and one of my other great-grandfathers died in a corn shop. My father was a salaried, year-round shop superintendent when he passed away in 1956. My mother worked in both the cookhouse and shop. I worked only one year, 1957, and that was only for three weeks. I was 16 at the time and the corn shops were on their way out."[9]

Clyde Davis of Norway, Maine, also entered the business by way of his family's involvement with the Burnham & Morrill Company:

> "My folks were associated with the B & M plant in Auburn, Maine, and also grew corn for the cannery and produced seed. I had worked there a little in 1941-42 as a part-time general laborer before going into the service. After returning to Auburn, I got hurt and became somewhat of a straw boss at the corn shop. The next year, 1947, I was transferred to South Paris, Maine, to manage that plant. The old factory there burned

in 1943 and its replacement was a year round set-up that processed pork and beans as well as other products. As manager I worked an average of 40 hours per week and received a paycheck of $50-55. The wages were satisfactory but after a few years I thought I might quit and do something else. But then I realized that I was getting older and wasn't going to college. So I changed my mind and decided to stay. At least I knew the business!

In 1966 B & M sold out to William Underwood Company, but Underwood was not interested in retaining the South Paris factory and it was purchased by A. L. Stewart Company. Stewart dropped the corn line but continued to pack applesauce, wax beans, blueberries and potatoes. I stayed on with the new owner and eventually retired after 37 years in the canning business. It was fun but bugs and weather were constant worries.[10]

New Portland, Maine, farmer Marshall Edwards had established a reputation for raising excellent corn for canning. A bout with polio had limited his ability to do hard physical work. I knew him as a family friend, and we often discussed the sweet corn business before his passing:

"I went to Starks in 1947 to replace Ralph Soule as superintendent of the corn shop there. My wife Evelyn and I had gone to Portland in the winter of 1947 to meet with Monmouth Canning Company officials about the position. We felt it might be a good move because of my polio problem. We agreed to take the job and soon moved into the company house in Starks. The shop processed only sweet corn and was in good running order. My salary was about $5,200 per year and the annual factory payroll was around $50,000. During the first year my field man, Claude Mitchell, died and I had to take on that duty. My formal education had ended with graduation from Central High School in New Portland, Maine; however, crop farming experience and sound management skills gave me a pretty solid background to run the corn shop. I stayed at the job until the place closed in 1963.[11]

Superintendents came from a variety of backgrounds. Some worked their way up through the canning industry while others were recruited directly from the farm. This mix once again highlights the importance of production skills and quality control in both field and factory operations.

Workers

Below management, the industry's labor force included a few people that were employed year round. In the early years of the business some would have been making cans and boxes for the packing season; but, by the post-World War One period most of those jobs were displaced by new can making machines and cardboard cases. Limited non-canning season opportunities would continue - labeling, shipping, trucking and for those companies growing some of their own crops, fieldwork in summer.

During 2000, I interviewed sixty-five former corn shop workers in Maine, New Hampshire and Vermont to document their social and economic characteristics and produce a profile of the laborers in the industry. These workers represent 23 different canneries scattered among 19 towns in the three states. About 80 percent of the sample workers and associated shops were in Maine (Tables 6.1 and 6.2). Gender distribution of former workers is about fifty-five percent male and 45 percent female (Table 6.3). One would expect most of the people interviewed to have worked during the latter years of the "corn shop century" (Table 6.4). Many of the workers of pre-World War Two have passed away and by the 1960's, few shops were left. One worker started before 1920. All job assignments that existed in a post-World War One corn shop are represented in the sample worker population (Table 6.5). Most workers would have experience in more than a single job. About a quarter of the people had worked as a husker feeder, belt inspector or labeler. Other categories with relatively high numbers were cutter feeder, can feeder, retort foreman, bath waterman, packing room laborer and general laborer.

Tasks were often aligned by gender. Lifting, high temperatures and jobs that required a fair amount of moving around (mixing, retort activity, bath water operation and laborers), were largely male, whereas women were usually at stationary repetitive positions (husker feeder, inspection belt, cutter feeder and can feeder). Some assignments such as labeling had little relationship to gender. Most of the workplace was either male or female space.

In general, people did not have long careers in corn shops. Employees averaged 6.8 seasons with women having a bit more staying power than men (Table 6.6). On the other hand, men tended to start at a younger age than women. More than a third of the males began work

N = 65	
Maine	83.0%
New Hampshire	4.5%
Vermont	11.0%
Others	1.5%

Table 6.1   Current Residence of Former Corn Shop Workers Interviewed by Author. *Source:* Author's Survey.

N = 65	
Maine	81.5%
New Hampshire	6.2%
Vermont	12.3%

Table 6.2   Location of Canneries that Employed Workers Interviewed by Author - (23 Canneries in 19 different towns). *Source:* Author's Survey.

N = 65	
Male	55.4%
Female	44.6%

Table 6.3   Gender of Workers Interviewed by Author. *Source:*Author's Survey.

N = 65						
	1910's	1920's	1930's	1940's	1950's	1960's
Male	1	1	10	20	24	15
Female	0	2	7	16	21	9
Total	1	3	17	36	45	24

Table 6.4   Decades in Which Interviewees Worked in Corn Canneries. Note: Some workers worked in more than one decade. *Source:* Author's Survey.

Job	Male	Female	All (Total)
Bookkeeper	1 (2.8%)	2 (6.9%)	3 (4.6%)
Weigh master	0	3 (10.3%)	3 (4.6%)
Yardmaster	2 (5.6%)	0	2 (3.1%)
Tester	0	1 (3.4%)	1 (1.5%)
Husker Foreman	2 (5.6%)	0	2 (3.1%)
Husker Feeder	1 (2.8%)	16 (55.2%)	17 (26.2%)
Belt Inspector	0	16 (55.2%)	16 (24.6%)
Cutter Foreman	1 (2.8%)	0	1 (1.5%)
Cutter Feeder	1 (2.8%)	7 (24.1%)	8 (12.3%)
Syrup Mixer	4 (11.1%)	0	4 (6.2%)
Corn Mixer	3 (8.3%)	1 (3.4%)	4 (6.2%)
Cooker Machinist	2 (5.6%)	1 (3.4%)	3 (4.6%)
Canner Machinist	3 (8.3%)	0	3 (4.6%)
Can Feeder	2 (5.6%)	5 (17.2%)	7 (10.8%)
Filler	2 (5.6%)	0	2 (3.1%)
Capper	1 (2.8%)	0	1 (1.5%)
Retort Foreman	8 (22.2%)	0	8 (12.3%)
Bath Waterman	7 (19.4%)	0	7 (10.8%)
Fireman	2 (5.6%)	0	2 (3.1%)
Machinist Helper	1 (2.8%)	0	1 (1.5%)
Boxer	2 (5.6%)	2 (6.9%)	4 (6.2%)
Warehouse Laborer	5 (13.9%)	1 (3.4%)	6 (9.2%)
Packing Room Laborer	8 (22.2%)	2 (6.9%)	10 (15.4%)
Labeler	9 (25.0%)	6 (20.7%)	15 (23.1%)
Labeling Machinist	1 (2.8%)	0	1 (1.5%)
General Laborer	10 (27.8%)	2 (6.9%)	12 (18.5%)
Other	3 (8.3%)	0	3 (4.6%)

Table 6.5   Job Assignments of Cannery Workers. Note: Most workers had more than one job during their time at the shops. *Source:* Author's Survey.

before they were 16 years old (Table 6.7). Parents and company
management appear to have been inclined to let boys rather than girls
slide into the workplace as child labor. On average, men had completed
their corn shop years by age 24 and women by age 28 (Table 6.8). This
pattern may reflect the mobility of men to move on to other
opportunities while women by their early 20's were probably married
with children and had little chance for jobs outside. Men tended to
have less education than women when beginning at the shop, but their
education as adults was equal to the women (Table 6.9 and 6.10). The
limited sample and the extended spread from World War One to the
1960's makes a wage evaluation a bit challenging. Men were paid more
than women (Table 6.11). The general policy of linking the shop pay to
Maine and U.S. minimum wage was recognized by both workers and
management. The first Federal minimum wage was 25 cents per hour
set in 1938. By the mid-1960's, it had reached $1.25 while Maine's
minimum at that time was $1.15.[12] Modest hourly rates could be offset
by working long hours, which many did. The typical work day during
canning season was over eleven hours with men putting in longer ones
(Table 6.12). Men also worked a few more days per season than
women (Table 6.13). In those canneries where other foods were
processed, men were more likely to extend their work season than
women (Table 6.14). About half the labor force came from households
that also grew crops for the canneries (Table 6.15). These people often
had both field and shop duties during the hectic processing season.

   Most of the workers lived close to the shop with about 50 percent
within two miles and few traveling more than six miles to work (Figure
6.1). Females tended to cluster nearer to the shop. Over half of the
employees often walked to work and driving was also common,
especially for men (Table 6.16). This journey to work pattern is
expected, considering the pre-driver license age of many workers, lower
driving rates for women during the 40's and 50's, modest wage scale
and long shifts.

   Workers represented a broad economic and social spectrum. As
noted by Alfred Hurwitz in his *History of Liberty Maine 1827-1995,*
"The factory was a great leveler of status, for no woman in town
considered herself above working there."[13] The majority of women were
married at some time during their employment, whereas only a quarter
of the men had that status while working at a corn shop (Table 6.17).
Men frequently had their canning adventure behind them before they wed.

N = 65	
Male	5.1 (Range = 1-20)
Female	8.1 (Range = 1-32)
All	6.8 (Range = 1-32)

Table 6.6   Average Number of Seasons Worked by Employees. *Source:* Author's Survey.

N = 63	
Male	36.1%
Female	20.7%
All	29.2%

Table 6.7   Percent of Workers Employed Before Age 16. *Source:* Author's Survey.

N = 60	
Male	23.9 (Range = 15-60)
Female	28.3 (Range = 17-59)
All	25.7 (Range = 15-60)

Table 6.8   Average Age When Employees Ceased Working in Canneries. *Source:* Author's Survey.

N = 57			
	Male	Female	All
Yes	11 (37.9%)	18 (64.3%)	29 (51%)
No	18 (62.1%)	10 (35.7%)	28 (49%)

Table 6.9   Number of Employees Completing Grade 12 Before Starting Work in Canneries. *Source:* Author's Survey.

N = 60	
Male	13.0
Female	12.4
All	12.6

Table 6.10   Average Years of Education Eventually Completed by Cannery Workers. *Source:* Author's Survey.

N = 48	
Male	$ .69
Female	$ .52
All	$ .63

Table 6.11   Cannery Workers Average Wage Per Hour. *Source:* Author's Survey.

N = 61	
Male	12.4
Female	10.2
All	11.2

Table 6.12   Average Hours Cannery Employees Worked Per Day.   *Source:* Author's Survey.

N = 64	
Male	40.1
Female	37.9
All	39.1

Table 6.13   Average Number of Days Worked Per Year Canning Corn. *Source:* Author's Survey.

N = 39	
Male	24 (61.5%)
Female	15 (38.5%)

Table 6.14   Number of Corn Shop Workers Who Processed Other Vegetables. *Source:* Author's Survey.

N = 65	
Male	21 (58.3%)
Female	15 (51.7%)
All	36 (55.4%)

Table 6.15   Number of Cannery Workers Whose Households Grew Crops for Canneries. *Source:* Author's Survey.

N = 57			
Mode	Male	Female	All
Drive	23 (63.9%)	10 (34.5%)	33 (50.1%)
Walk	19 (52.8%)	16 (55.2%)	35 (53.8%)
Ride with another person	6 (16.7%)	5 (17.2%)	11 (16.9%)
Company bus	1 (2.8%)	1 (3.4%)	2 (3.1%)
Other	0	1 (3.4%)	1 (1.5%)

Table 6.16   Cannery Workers' Mode of Transportation to Work. Note: Some Workers used more than one mode. *Source:* Author's Survey.

N = 62	
Male	25.0%
Female	58.6%
All	42.1%

Table 6.17   Percent of Employees Married. *Source:* Author's Survey.

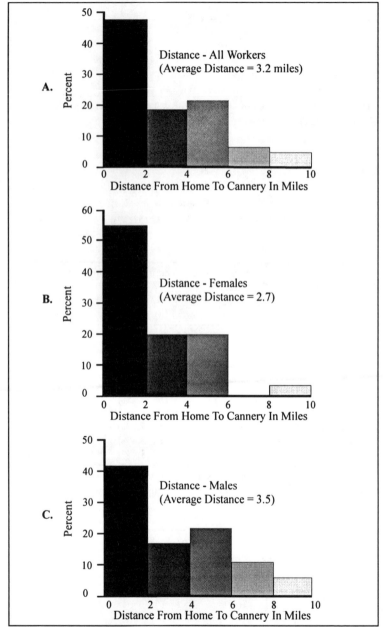

Figure 6.1   Distance from Home to Cannery. *Source:* Author's Survey.

Comfort in the workplace and job satisfaction were important considerations to most people. Safety in the corn shop was not a major concern. Protective clothing was available and often worn (Table 6.18). Although there were many potential injury-inflicting machines, most people stayed out of harm's way. Pay was the least satisfactory aspect of the corn shop experience, although the long work hours were a close second (Table 6.19). The social atmosphere at the shops was attractive to most people because they were working with their friends (Table 6.20). For both men and women, child care was often a problem. Organized day care was not common and most arrangements were with family or neighbors. Bringing children to work was sometimes the only choice (Table 6.21).

In the end, the paycheck came into the household budget. The money was pretty well spread around with general household and school needs taking much of it (Table 6.22). I recall that children frequently started the school year with old clothes, but by the second or third week of classes after a corn shop check or two, new shoes, dresses and shirts would appear. Real estate tax bills usually arrived in the mail box at about the end of the canning season. Among men, "other" was a significant expenditure. Teenager male recreational needs may have skewed this variable.

The Corn Shop is Running

Survey data present an overall impression of corn shop workers. In-depth recollections add insight, personality and warmth to the collective experiences. In mid-to-late August word would spread quickly that "the corn shop is running" and much of the community would respond. A range of perceptions and memories are included among the folks that canned the gold. Each work station in a typical shop is represented in the following interviews (Figure 5.2).

Upon arrival at the cannery the farmer might encounter a bit of congestion as a line formed at the scales. Yardmasters, like Arthur Hill, made sure that traffic bringing corn in and taking waste away moved without delays. About the only problems would be farmers trying to jump ahead in line or trucks getting stuck in muddy yards. Hill began work in the Baxter plant in North Fryeburg, Maine, as an 11- year-old hand husker in 1918. He performed many different tasks in the Fryeburg canneries until 1965 when the last one in the area closed.[14]

N = 65			
Clothing	Male	Female	All
Head Cover	4 (10.3%)	5 (13.2%)	9 (13.8%)
Gloves	12 (30.8%)	6 (15.8%)	18 (27.7%)
Boots	4 (10.4%)	2 (5.3%)	6 (9.2%)
Apron	15 (38.5%)	14 (36.8%)	29 (44.6%)
Overalls	4 (10.3%)	3 (7.9%)	7 (10.8%)
Total	39	30	69

Table 6.18   Protective Clothing Worn. *Source:* Author's Survey.

N = 65		
Variable	Male	Female
Pay	3	3
Work hours	3.5	3
Seasonal nature	3.5	4
People worked with	5	5
Safety in the workplace	4	4
Nearness to home	5	5

Table 6.19   Job Satisfaction Level (Rank 1-5 with 5 highest).*Source:* Author's Survey.

N = 65	
Male	33 Yes (91.7%)
Female	24 Yes (82.8%)
All	57 Yes (87.7%)

Table 6.20   Socialized With Other Workers. *Source:* Author's Survey.

N = 65			
Option	Male	Female	All
Older children	4	3	7 (33.8%)
Grandparents	2	2	4 (21.1%)
Neighbor	6	5	11 (57.9%)
Organized daycare	0	0	0 (0.0%)
Other (including bringing child to work)	9	9	18 (94.7%)

Table 6.21   How Did You Provide Child Care (If Needed)? *Source:* Author's Survey.

N = 65			
Item	Male	Female	All
General Household	17 (47.2%)	14 (48.3%)	31 (47.0%)
School needs for children	10 (27.8%)	11 (42.3%)	21 (33.3%)
TAXES Real Estate	4 (11.1%)	1 (3.4%)	5 (7.7%)
Other	25 (69.4%)	10 (34.5%)	35 (53.8%)

Table 6.22   How Corn Shop Wages Were Spent. *Source:* Author's Survey.

The grower pulled his wagon or truck onto the scales, and the weigh-master recorded the tonnage. After unloading, the empty rig was reweighed and the difference was the farmer's corn weight. Eula Knowlton was a weighmaster for the Monmouth factory in Freedom, Maine. She had grown up in a corn shop family and hired on as a 15 year old husker feeder at the Portland Packing Company cannery in Albion, Maine, in 1940. During the Second World War, her father managed the German POW's at the shop in Albion. Later, Knowlton worked five seasons in Freedom, where the most enjoyable shop entertainment was discussing who was courting whom and stories about bootlegging booze.[15]

Bookkeeping for corn payment, payroll and other bills and running the scales were performed sometimes by the same person. Thelma Bean carried out these tasks at the Monmouth shop in Starks from 1958-63. She was a local, single woman in her 20's living only three miles from the cannery. Bean's duties were year round with full work weeks during planting, growing and canning seasons, May to October. The remainder of the year involved one day per week. There were few arguments in the business office except for an occasional disagreement over time worked in the shop. Some people claimed longer hours than they should have.[16]

After the corn was unloaded, it was tested for quality. This, combined with weight, determined what farmers would be paid. Evangline Matijczyk, a college girl, worked as a tester at the Baxter Brothers plant in Corinna, Maine, for two summers, 1944-45. That facility had just been converted to a freezing operation, however, Baxter still canned in nearby Hartland. Evangline tested peas, beans and corn. The better produce went into frozen lines, whereas the poorer quality vegetables were reloaded and sent to the Hartland shop. Farmers had an incentive to deliver good quality because they got paid more for better vegetables that were satisfactory for freezing. Evangeline's job was a clean one and it helped pay for her university education. The best part of her employment was meeting her soldier, a POW guard, who later became her husband. "I tell people I had a choice, him or a German POW, and they were all officers!" [17]

Young laborers were often found in the open sheds hoeing corn into conveyor chains that carried it to the husking room. Stanley Linscott was a teenager during his two seasons, 1935-36, of work for Burnham & Morrill in Cornish, Maine. In the summer he hoed corn for farmers and then hoed it into the conveyors during canning season. He received his social security number while working at the shop.[18] Lawrence Day served as husking room foreman for one year in the late 1940's at the Medomak cannery in New Sharon and notes that long hours were required. His wife also worked at the shop. They purchased a hardware store and did not work in the cannery after 1949.[19]

Feeding a husking machine required the operator to stand or sit on a tall stool at the same work station for hours at a time. Nearly all feeders were women. Pauline Wyman was 18 during her one five-week season in 1950 at the Monmouth shop in Starks. She recalls, "I ran a husker across from one that my mother was at, which was nice. All the ears had to be headed into the machinery in the same direction. The floor was always wet and it was easy to slip."[20]

Following removal of the husks, the ears traveled along a belt for inspection. Grubs and damaged corn had to be cut away. This tedious task was considered one of the least desirable assignments. Women worked on the belt and it was often the young that found themselves there. Loraine Hodges spent two seasons in corn shops in Farmington, Maine, 1952 for Franklin Farms and 1953 for Burnham & Morrill. As a 16-year-old, she confronted motion sickness caused by the continuous belt. It was her first experience working around machinery. The most fun about the job was playing ball with the other employees when there was a breakdown.[21]

The ears were then washed before moving to cutters. Sayward Hackett, who began working as a 12 year old at the Starks factory in 1945, finished his corn canning career in 1953. He spent much of his life on the so called "wet end" washing the ears with cold water where long, cold, wet days and nights were certain. Ralph Soule, shop superintendent at that time, provided a company truck to transport people from nearby Industry, Maine, where Hackett lived, to Starks. This made it possible for him to work. He remembers being afraid of the POW's and the guards with guns. There were 15-20 POW's at the Starks factory in 1945. They worked throughout the cannery but were always visible and at stationary jobs.[22]

The cutter feeders were mainly women, and there was little chance to move around. Gladys Lovell began working at the Medomak shop in New Sharon, Maine, at age 16 in 1929 and was there for the 1930, 31 and 32 seasons as well. Lovell was on the belt those years but after moving to Starks, getting married and having six children, her corn shop career picked up again. From 1960 to 63, she was a cutter feeder for Monmouth's Starks' cannery. It was a messy operation requiring constant feeding of corn into a machine with rotating knives. She wore an apron and hair net to protect her from juice that flew from the fast moving blades as they cleaned the cobs. When she was not at the corn shop, she worked as a mid-wife.[23] Edgar Reed, who began working for Leonard Packing Company (later B & M), in Pittsfield, New Hampshire, in 1930 and continued to take seasonal jobs with the factory until its closure in 1965, once traded jobs with a woman on a cutter to giver her a break for a short time.[24] To see a man in this female job appears to have been an unusual event.

Following its passage through the cutters, corn entered the desilker where a series of mesh screens removed bits of husk, cob and silk. As a college student in the early 1960's, Rodney Porter worked in both the New Sharon, Maine, Medomak shop and the Franklin Farms cannery in Farmington, Maine. He was assigned to different jobs and ran the desilker at Farmington. It was a busy work environment and breaks were difficult to get. All the belts and gears were open and from time to time someone would tap a belt causing it to run off its pulley. This resulted in a little rest until maintenance men came around and put it back on. Long shifts and repetition were always part of the job. Porter never could see how women were able to work on the inspection belt for hours. He tried it one day. Watching corn move along drove him nuts! Porter recalled the social skill-building character of corn shops. "Because I was a young college kid sometimes a few of the older women would say things that they thought would corrupt my mind a little. I did learn to swear pretty well and was asked to tone it down when I went into the army. Corn shops had quality swearing!" Porter remembers that weekly pay was good because of the long shifts and that Richard Gould, owner of Franklin Farms, was a wonderful boss.[25]

At ages 17 and 18, Austin Wood worked two season 1939-40, mixing syrup at the Demeritt plant in Randolph, Vermont. His brother had been a syrup mixer before him.

> The shop would start canning at about 10:00 in the morning and work often ran 10-12 hours. There was only one shift and it ran until the corn was canned. "We canned only corn but did both whole and cream style. I used to make different syrups. If the corn was going to S. S. Pierce (high end of the market), I would make it thicker than if it was on A & P (mid-market) order. S. S. Pierce would have a bit more sugar and a

little more flour. If the shop was going to can for A & P all day, we would go light on the syrup. On the other hand, if the day started out for S. S. Pierce then switched to A & P, the mix probably wouldn't be changed. There was some enjoyment at the shop and I remember it was fun to watch the capper. After I made the syrup, which was an upstairs operation, I would go part way downstairs so I could watch the capper. It would wang and wang putting on can covers. The least enjoyable thing was to hear that another load of corn was coming in after you had planned to go home. I spent much of my corn shop wage taking a girl out on Saturday night. It was 11 cents to go to the movies then."[26]

After the syrup had been prepared, it was mixed with the corn. James Warren and his wife Almora, both worked at the B & M factory in Pittsfield, New Hampshire, from the 1940's into the 60's. Each performed many different cannery jobs and corn mixer was something they both did. Long hours were a challenge but they were able to fulfill their shop responsibilities as well as run a farm and butcher shop. Their daughter also worked at the cannery. They recall that high school kids pretty much ran the factory at night. Students came in after classes and the adults went home.[27]

In 1943 Orland Seamon was one of nine children living on the family farm in Jay, Maine, when he was hired at age 13 to work in the Thomas and Marble Company corn cannery in the Dryden section of Wilton, Maine. His father milked about a dozen cows and grew beans, cucumbers and corn for the B & M factory in Livermore Falls, Maine. The kids were all encouraged to get off-farm jobs whenever they could. During World War Two children as young as 12 could be hired if they had permission from their parents. His brother also worked for Thomas and Marble. Years later, Seamon worked a few days in the New Sharon shop once just so he could see his girlfriend (future wife) who worked there. It was more of a courting activity than a job. In the early 60's while employed at Franklin Farms as the night cooker, he was also working days as a hand sewer in a shoe shop. "I had to make sure that the cooker temperature was 190 degrees. Mr. Gould (the boss) would often look over my shoulder to check the gauge. I worked about 10 hour shifts." [28]

From the cooker vat, corn was transferred to cans which were being fed to the filler by a can feeder such as Barbara McGrath. She worked at the Demeritt cannery in Waterbury, Vermont, from 1938 to the 1960's. During the off season, Demeritt hired her at his wood products plant. Accurate filling and dependable capping of the cans required a smooth flow of empties from the feeder. On one occasion, the shop crew was rushing through the last of the day's pack so they could attend the Tunbridge (Vermont) Fair which is always held in mid-September. McGrath fouled up the feeding and the whole shop shut down until the mess was fixed. She wasn't very popular that night![29]

From 1941 to 1948, Glen Fitch, a young man, performed a variety of tasks including filling cans at the Medomak operation in New Sharon. He recalls long hours, a fair amount of drinking from bottles hidden around the shop and spending much of his paycheck chasing women. Because his father grew vegetables for the factory, Glen also had field work to do.[30]

Peter Mills II worked as a 20-year-old capper for Franklin Farms in Farmington. He recalls, "I worked at the shop to earn money for college. Most of the workforce (1963 season) was made up of women. It was like working in a museum with antique equipment. Sleep deprivation was the hardest part of the job."[31]

After the cans were sealed, they advanced in line to a level surface where a person used a hand strap to pull them onto trays which were stacked for transport to the retort room and additional cooking under pressure. Stanley Nightingale did strapping, among other duties, at the Medomak plant in New Sharon during the 1950's. While a teenager before going to Medomak, he had some experience at the Monmouth cannery in Starks. When not working in the cannery plants, he did lumbering, general farm labor and served on a state road tar crew. He was not married and thinks most of his money went to school needs and dating women.[32]

Lloyd Perkins ran retorts for Franklin Farms in Farmington in 1961 and 62. He took the cans out of the retorts and transferred them to the water bath station. It was largely the night shift and involved about 10 hours of work per day. Perkins got home in time to sleep a little before going to work haying for farmers during the day. He received minimum wage, about $1.05 per hour, at the shop. His family also grew sweet corn for canning. In 1963 he went into the service and remembers when getting ready for discharge, writing to Richard Gould, owner of Franklin Farms, and asking him about a job at the cannery again. "I said any position except the retort area was just fine. After being in 104 degrees temperatures in Vietnam, I didn't think I wanted to go back to the retorts!" [33]

Robert Abare served as bath waterman for Demeritt's facility in Waterbury, Vermont, and like many of the cannery employees, he also worked in Demeritt's clothespin plant. His tenure, 1938-47, at the cooling station and on other canning jobs exposed him to a variety of unusual things. He recalls that practical jokes were common and once saw a corn borer with red fingernail polish on its nose go into a can of corn.[34]

Steam was critical for cooking, retort and cleaning operations at the shops. Clarence Holbrook worked as an engineer (fireman) at J. W. Bennett's Lakeside Packing Company in the northern part of Auburn, Maine. This was a small family business that canned a number of vegetables and fruits. Some were for the commercial market and custom canning was a big part of the enterprise. About 15-20 people were employed. Holbrook started work there about 1942 as a 12 year old and continued until 1952. He liked working with steam and was sure to wear good gloves. The least enjoyable aspect of the job was cleaning up machines at the end of the day. Holdbrook thinks he spent a fair amount of his cannery money on fishing equipment. Following his canning career, he attended technical college in Chicago and later worked in the shoe industry.[35]

Cooled cans moved on to the packing room where a boxer would staple cardboard cartons into shape before the product was cased up. One of John Currier's jobs at the New Sharon Medomak factory was boxer. He worked there for the 1942, 43 and 44 seasons. Currier was in high school at that time and was busy during both bean and corn seasons. After school started in September, Currier cut back his time to weekends. Most work days were 10-12 hours. His childhood was spent on a farm where his father planted beans and corn, about 3 acres of each, for the cannery. Young Currier also had jobs working in the woods, especially peeling pulp. Before powerful debarking machines were installed in pulp mills, buyers paid a premium for peeled pulp. The cannery was a busy place with a lot of food-stuffs being processed-apples, corn, beans, blueberries, squash and fish. Fish were a little unusual. New Sharon is about 70 miles from the coast, but Meadomak had a problem getting all its fish inventory canned in its coastal factory and therefore trucked the highly perishable product to the inland vegetable shop for canning. That practice didn't last long. Currier thinks that most of his corn shop paychecks were spent on clothes and candy for his girlfriend. It must have been good candy; she has been with him for 52 years! [36]

Don Welch, another of Roy Demeritt's employees that made clothespins and canned vegetables, worked as a packing room laborer during the 1958 and 59 seasons in Waterbury, Vermont. His wage at that time was about $38 per week and it came as cash in a brown envelope on Friday nights.[37]

Each unsealed case of produce would be moved to the warehouse for storage until purchase orders arrived. Dennis Brown worked in the warehouse at the Medomak factory in New Sharon, Maine, from 1955 until it burned in 1960. He started out in high school and continued while attending college. Brown is now chairman of the Biochemistry Department at North Carolina State University and thinks that his corn shop career made him a better man. "Drinking and bullshitting were aspects of the cannery environment and the operation was a real part of the community."[38]

A little labeling might be done during packing season; but most of that activity was scattered throughout the year as orders arrived. Major brand names were attached to most cans (Table 5.8). Edward Conant worked as a labeler, and at other jobs at the Demeritt shop in Randolph, Vermont. He recalls that the factory would sometimes run out of corn and close until more was ready to can. Once, there was a 10-acre field of good corn that was not quite ripe and the shop had to wait for it. The company gave a prize to the farmer that grew the best corn. POW's were used at the shop and a Mrs. Bell housed them in Randolph. One practical joke was to put a mud turtle on the belt and watch the women inspecting the corn, scatter.[39]

Workers that kept the canneries going often engaged in both field and factory jobs as well as filling other roles both in and outside the canning community. Ina Porter Turner of Farmington, Maine, is fairly typical of a "corn shop girl," as women employees were often called. Turner is the person that could hear cans exploding from her home in Farmington Falls when the New Sharon factory burned (p. 85). Her recall about sweet corn processing began with observations as a twenty year old and continues into middle age. If I had to nominate someone for the honor of typical corn shop worker, Turner would be seriously considered.

Turner worked at both the B & M plant at Farmington Falls and Medomak's operation in New Sharon as well as picking corn. Thirteen seasons (1935-36 and 1949-60) were covered by her career, with a few while unmarried just after high school and a longer period as a housewife with family. Turner fed the belt and did labeling.

I remember that George McKeene managed the B & M plant when I worked there and it was the cleanest corn shop I have ever seen. One time when I was employed there the fireman got the boiler firebox too hot because he used too much dry wood. My father was called from across the river to see if he could help cool it down. He put on heavy leather gloves and pulled fire out of the box and saved the day.

At the New Sharon shop I worked 7 to 8 hours each day, but, after we had kids, I sometimes had to get home early to take care of them. We lived on Cape Cod Hill, two miles from the cannery, and drove to work. I worked 2-3 weeks on squash. The job was good because of the hours, seasonal nature, nice people and nearness to home. I don't remember what we got paid, but it wasn't a hell of a lot. I wore gloves and an apron at work and know the corn juice was hard to clean off. The pay check went to general household needs and for school supplies. We had five children and hired a neighborhood girl, Hattie Rackcliff, to babysit until our oldest child was old enough to sit. We paid $5-6 per week. Our kids picked beans for the shop when they were big enough and I also picked corn. One woman that was sometimes picking corn with me was as large as a door. She would pick two rows at a time and one could always tell where she had been because her broad behind would knock over both rows.

Our family never grew crops for the shops and I didn't have a regular job. When the cannery wasn't running we fished a lot and ate what was caught. We were glad when the corn shop job came around and a dollar could be earned.[40]

Frank Brown, father of Dennis the warehouse laborer, is representative of the bond that developed between corn shops and the larger community. Although his employment in canning lasted only a few years, 1935-38, he was in contact with the industry from childhood until age 40 when, in 1960, the New Sharon, Maine, factory burned. Most of his adult years were spent managing a farm supply store and serving as town road foreman or fire chief. In the late 1920's, the Browns moved from New Brunswick, Canada, to a farm in the Cape Cod Hill neighborhood of New Sharon. The family grew beans, corn and squash for local canneries. Frank was one of nine children and remembers, at age 11, working in his father's field and for nearby farmers.

"We got half-a-cent per pound for picking beans but the money went to our parents. We weren't allowed to have money. Harvey Harderson, a neighboring farmer, didn't pay us anything. We had recently moved from Canada and over there kids didn't handle money. We were little slaves! I can remember Dad telling Harvey, 'Don't you pay those kids a damn cent. They don't work for anything. They are suppose to help people.' Harvey said, 'We have to pay them something.' So on Saturday night he would load us onto the back of his truck and take us to Farmington Falls and buy us all the ice cream we wanted.

I hoed corn for Clarence Drown, who had a large field next to the Sandy River and would take my lunch to work in the morning and set it down next to the road. By the time I hoed the length of the field and back to the road, it was time for lunch. Pulling witchgrass was also part of the job.

Will Works, another local farmer who was considered a tight manager and was allegedly able to milk money out of a tree, would hire me to pick corn. He wanted me to pick at 2:00 a.m. because it had dew on it and would weight more when delivered to the shop. He paid me $1 each time I picked for him. Imagine getting up at 2 in the morning to pick corn! Mr. Works had a hernia that would pop out sometimes, and he would lay down between the corn rows and put it back himself. Oh, it was quite an education.

In 1935 I was hired at the B & M shop in Farmington Falls and received my social security number at that time. I did odd jobs there which included wheeling wood to the boiler room. During the 1936, 37 and 38 seasons, I worked for the Medomak cannery in New Sharon. My father often hunted with members of the Bird family that owned the company and that helped me land the job. I worked in the packing room and served as night watchman and stayed on the full season; two weeks on beans, five on corn and two on squash for a total of nine. The average work day was 12-14 hours and the shop ran all night. There were no set shifts and pay was about $.25 per hour. At the time I could get $.50 per day working for a farmer, thus the shop wage looked pretty good.

I lived about 3 miles from the cannery and had an arrangement with another neighbor farmer, Bert Sawyer, which made it possible to drive my father's truck to work. Bert would pay me $25 for each load of corn waste I delivered to him. Dad had a truck that I drove to the shop and I would park in the yard. After other farmers had taken their turn at loading waste, one of the men working in the yard would set the truck under the waste chute and fill it for me. After it was full, they would drive it out of the way. When my shift was over, I drove it to Mr. Sawyer's farm. I thought $25 was a lot for pay but Bert claimed it would come out in the milk.

The canneries were interesting places to work. Safety and quality control were not high priorities. There were a lot of open belts and gears and some workers received a few burns in the retort area but there were not many serious accidents. I once saw Pearly Caswell drop an oil can into the corn vat where the corn and syrup are mixed and I asked him what he was going to do about it. Pearly said, 'nothing, it will get mixed and only a little oil will be in each can.' I spent much of my corn shop pay on education. My plan was to become a public accountant and I enrolled in a correspondence course. However, I never thought about the cannery job coming to an end. When it did I decided to get income to cover the course by shooting hedgehogs. I got $.25 per hedgehog by cutting off the feet and nose and taking them to Bounty Agent, Pearly Caswell. Unfortunately, I ran out of hedgehogs and money and wasn't able to finish the course. I still have the books. The correspondence school also had me keeping books for a business in Ohio. I wanted to go to the college so bad, but we were just too damn poor. I don't blame my parents, there were nine kids.

After a hitch in the Army, I returned to New Sharon. Although I never went back into the canneries, my contact with sweet corn didn't come to an end. In the early 1950's, I was foreman of a town road crew and one year was doing late summer repairs near the Archie Davis farm. Davis was growing corn for the Starks cannery and Marshall Edwards, the Starks shop superintendent, had discovered that the Davis' field was close to being too ripe. Edwards had alerted farmer Davis and they were desperate to find pickers to harvest it. Edwards encountered my highway workers and convinced me to pull the men off the road project and have them pick. Edwards, who had a physical disability, would drive the truck while we picked and carried baskets of ears to it as it moved along through the field. However, his foot was heavy on the gas and it wasn't possible for the pickers to keep up with the truck. The men complained and asked Edwards to slow down; however, there was no reduction in speed. When the operation reached the end of the row, I told my crew members to turn their baskets over and sit on them. Edwards headed the truck back into the corn but soon realized that no one was picking. While an argument about the relationship between truck and picker speeds was starting to warm up, Davis drove up and wanted to know what the trouble was. I told him we had plenty of road work to do and weren't going to run after a truck. After some discussion Davis agreed to replace Edwards at the wheel and the corn got picked.

I was town fire chief at the time the New Sharon shop burned in 1960 and knew that the loss of buildings and season's pack represented several million dollars, a large sum for that time. Some of the cans were salvaged and reboxed at the Starks factory. I recall, 'We were always glad when the

shop opened in the summer and were happy when it closed at the end of
the season. But, we were dammed sorry when the thing burned!" [41]

Others, although not directly paid as a grower or factory worker,
contributed to the success of the corn factories. Max Matijczyk was a
POW guard in 1944-45 and stationed in Bangor, Maine, where 250
prisoners were housed. He would transport them by truck to different
jobs; picking crops or working in canneries. Matijczyk had 15 POW's
at the Corinna, Maine, plant during corn season and some were sent to
the Hartland shop. They got paid a little. For picking beans, the
prisoners received 4 cents per pound with 2 cents going into a bank
account so that they would have a little money when they went back
home after the war. Matijczyk met a girl, Evangeline the tester, at the
Corinna plant and after his discharge, they were married. He obtained
a job at the local woolen mill and later worked as a cabinetmaker. [42]

This discussion has followed corn canning from field to label with
the thoughts of at least one person involved at each step along the way.
Various smells, sounds and feels encountered at a corn shop are difficult
to capture literally, but they are never forgotten. Fresh corn arriving in
the yard had a field odor that is experienced when walking next to
growing corn. A sweetness hung in the air where corn was cut and
cooked. There were always a few places where cleaning was not perfect
and the pungent air of fermentation revealed such spots. Putrid
effluvium and the deep yellow color of waterways downstream from
shops shocked the senses. Truck and tractor traffic, moving chains,
belts, drive gears, whirling knives, running water, steam release and
voices of men and women created a steady din. The splat of corn juice
followed by its stickiness, cold water, hot steam and slick floors were
all part of the feel. Late in the canning season (October) when night
temperatures were at or near freezing, extremes of hot versus cold in the
work environment were great. Employees endured temperature ranges
from freezing to roasting depending on the location of their work
stations. Everyone connected to canning corn experienced this
bombardment of odors, sights, sounds and feels.

Farmers, owners, superintendents and workers span the entire socio-
economic range of the population and they all played a role. Everyone
identified with the effort to deliver the end product. There was a certain
sense of community pride that came with a successful pack at the end
of the season.

Obituaries

When the last load has been canned it's time to clean up, reflect on the season and rest. The relentless passage of years has pushed "canners of gold" in the same direction as everyone else, toward the obituary listings and the big sabbatical. This reality was brought into sharp focus for me as I interviewed elderly former corn shop employees by day and browsed the obituaries at night. It was clear that the population of potential interviewees was shrinking at a noticeable pace. Some passed on soon after their interview. An obituary is the traditional last statement about an individual's life, revealing major details of a person's worldly adventure as well as philosophical insights. Although many went to their rewards without mention of the corn shop experience, not a surprise considering some of the recollections, a fair number of listings contain reference to corn canning jobs. A year's review, February 2000 to February 2001 of obituaries in the *Waterville (Maine) Morning Sentinel*, a central Maine daily, and the Farmington *(Maine) Franklin Journal,* a western Maine county semi-weekly, turned up 15 entries with mention of corn cannery careers (Table 6.23).

The average age of these people was 84 and canneries have been closed for a third of a century. Still, the memory of time at the corn factory was valued enough to be noted. Even the endurance of one corn shop romance is highlighted! Surely, there must be opportunities to can gold in heaven! The retorts probably blow out too often in the other place!

There Was A Corn Shop

Closure of a cannery threw many small farm communities into a crisis; no cash crop, no seasonal pay check, no waste for cattle feed, a vacant building and erosion of the tax base. Once a shop ceased operation it seldom restarted. Equipment frequently would be sold and removed for use at other canneries or sent into the scrap market. Farmers who had invested in mechanical pickers found themselves with equipment that was not in demand. Some turned to fodder corn for feed or tried dry beans as a cash crop. Workers did the best they could to find a substitute for lost income. Few options were available without a car to commute to a milltown or service center.

Community leaders sometimes undertook efforts to attract tenants to

Roseellen C. Hall - Fairfield Center, Maine; Age, 72; Death 2/11/00
"Roseellen was employed by Snowflake Canning Co. in Hartland..."

Florence Currier - Farmington, Maine; Age 88; Death 2/18/00
"In her earlier years she worked part-time for Foster Mfg. Co. in Strong and local corn factories."

Marshall W. Edwards - Farmington, Maine; Age 92; Death 2/22/00
"They (he and his wife Evelyn)...operated the family farm on New Portland Hill... producing maply syrup, timbering and growing string beans for the factory in Freedom and sweet corn for the Starks canning factory...They moved to Starks in 1947 where he accepted the position of superintendent of the Monmouth Canning Factory. At the close of the canning factory in 1963 he became a real estate agent."

Leona (Cyr) Emery - Hartland, Maine; Age 99; Death 2/24/00
"For many years, she was employed by Snowflake Canning Co., retiring in 1965."

Felta Lanpher - Palmyra, Maine; Age 92; Death 3/23/00
"For more than 30 years she worked at Baxter Canning Co. in Corinna, all the while helping her husband work the family farm."

Kenneth A. Brasier - Ripley, Maine; Age 72; Death 4/11/00
"After the service, he was employed in Dexter at the cannery, where he met his wife of 54 years, Nellie."

Maynard S. Stevens - Zephyrhills, Florida; Age 88; Death 4/30/00
"He owned (in Unity, ME)...a small restaurant known as The Shack, which operated only during the vegetable canning season."

Allen E. Bryson - Palmyra, Maine; Age 65; Death 6/22/00
"Allen was employed at Baxter Canning Co. in Corinna until it was destroyed by fire."

Maryland Knight - St. Albans, Maine; Age 77; Death 6/24/00
"He retired as a handsewer from Northeast Shoe Co. He was previously employed by Irving Tanning Co., and Snowflake Canning Co., as well as working in the woods."

Katherine M. Meader Lewis - Waterville, Maine; Age 82; Death 9/17/00
"She was employed by the corn factory in Albion, canning factory in Freedom, W.T. Grant in Waterville, and retired from Butler's Department store in Waterville."

Charlotte B. Crommett - Clinton, Maine; Age 103; Death 10/31/00
"In the late 1940's, she went to work during harvest time at the local canning factory for about 15 years."

Mary 'Agnes' Lenfest - Palmyra, Maine; Age 90; Death 12/14/00
"She was employed for many years by Snowflake Canning Co. in Corinna."

Norman L. Adams - New Sharon, Maine; Age 84; Death 1/14/01
"He was a lumberman for most of his life working in the surrounding area. He later worked in the local canning factories, retiring in the late 1960's.

Beatrice L. Conway - Newport, Maine; Age 80; Death 2/4/01
"She attended Corinna Union Academy and was employed for 20 years at Snowflake Canning Co. in Corinna."

Walter Thomas Nutter - Hartland, Maine; Age 80; Death 2/5/01
"Following his discharge in 1946, he was employed by Snowflake Canning Co. and H. C. Baxter and Son as an assistant plant manager. He joined the U.S. Postal Service in 1971 and retired as a rural carrier in 1986."

Table 6.23   Obituaries of Former Cannery Employees; Compiled by author. *Source: Waterville (Maine) Morning Sentinel* and *Farmington, (Maine) Franklin Journal.*

the vacated buildings, often without much success. These structures had been built to process a highly perishable agricultural product that has a large weight loss when canned. Thus, cannery density was high with many in little villages with small labor forces, poor roads, and no public sewer or water. There was no alternative to sweet corn canning and there was little demand for industrial space in many corn shop towns. The decision to close a shop or not rebuild after a fire was the prerogative of its owner, and, when word spread through the community, it was usually followed by both emotional and economic shock. When the Starks, Maine, shop closed in 1963, I recall my father, Glenn, remarking, "I can't imagine life without the corn shop." Much to the surprise of many, life went on! But, there seemed to be a big hole that never got filled, like an empty can. Those that have never seen anything but an empty can don't miss its contents.

Relics On The Landscape

I drove into Freedom Village, Maine, late one afternoon in early spring of 2000. It was a wonderful time to view the cultural landscape; most of the snow had gone and deciduous trees had not yet leafed out. Finding a spot to pull over on the soft shoulder without sinking to the hubcaps is a skill acquired over many years of driving in Northern New England during mud season. After searching for and finding solid ground to park and stand on, a glance through the hardwood trees that screened a valley revealed an irregular surface reflecting sunlight. A New England lake or pond on a windy day at "ice-out" time would give such an appearance. However, I knew it was the corn shop; a sprawling acre of steel and other roofing materials, sagging here, bulging there, pulling apart in another place. The Monmouth Canning Company had expanded the facility in the mid-1960's with plans to consolidate their corn and bean canning operation in a single shop. Soon after the plant was refitted, they sold out and the new owner, A. L. Stewart, did not find those products profitable. The building had been converted to a salvage, redemption and warehouse center and a seasonal thrift retail business. The access road was in marginal condition and there was no sign of recent activity. Little maintenance has been done and the whole setting gave a sense of rustic dishevelment (Figure 6.2).

The Pittsfield, New Hampshire, Burnham & Morrill corn factory stands on a side street. Since canning stopped in the mid-1960's, it has been managed as mixed use space with clothing manufacturing, leased storage, and auto repair bays (for locals with limited garage capacity). Little of the structure has been removed and it has been well maintained. A tour of the building reveals that much of the canning hardware is still in place; conveyor chains, gears, pulleys, drying spurs for locally grown seed corn, templates to label cases of corn, etc. A striking feature was the extensive corn shop graffiti proclaiming many romances that blossomed during the canning seasons. Sometimes the same name would appear carved into the center of more than one love heart with an arrow. Because the illustrations were undated, it's not possible to determine if the individuals noted had more than one involvement in a single season or if the art-work extended over several years with different sweethearts.[43] Documenting the details could be dangerous research!

The view from the geography classroom where I have taught for over 20 years at the University of Maine at Farmington includes a McDonald's restaurant and a gift shop. Until 1968 this site was occupied by the Franklin Farms corn factory, the last to can corn (under lease to Collins Foods) in Northern New England. Upon sale of the property by

Figure 6.2   Corn Shop, Freedom, Maine, 2000. *Source*: Author.

owner Richard Gould, it was razed except for a warehouse section. That was relocated to the back of the lot and is now the gift shop. McDonald's quickly built a restaurant on busy Intervale Road. The golden arches displaced cans of gold (Figure 6.3)!

From World War One until late summer of 2000, the Monmouth Canning Company corn shop on Chicken Street, stood like a mother hen watching over the village in Starks, Maine. Canning ceased in 1963 and the property passed through two farmers who used it for sorting and storing crops and equipment. The boiler house and one open shed was dismantled during that period. In the early 1980's, Starks Enterprises Corporation purchased the building with the intent of providing low cost space for small business start-ups. Some upgrade was done to the structure including a paint job that changed it from corn yellow to corn flower blue (Figure 6.4).

A variety of uses occupied parts of the building; automobile repair shop, woodworking factory, two general stores, bottle redemption center, nursery school, community library and lease storage. Building maintenance costs and insurance requirements necessitated the removal of more deteriorated parts of the structure. I acquired the remaining

Figure 6.3   Location of Former Cannery, Farmington, Maine, 2000. *Source:* Author.

Figure 6.4   Corn Shop, Starks, Maine, 1994. *Source*: Author.

open shed, moved it to the Frederic Farm, and it's now an equipment and hay storage area. In 1994 East Parish Housing, a church affiliated organization, bought the building and converted it into a thrift store handling clothing and household furnishings.[44] In 1995 the town celebrated its bicentennial by rallying around the old corn shop for the last time. It provided a great backdrop and much like any other retired citizen, it observed the merriment and maybe recalled past days of glory.

After pouring money into repair and maintenance, the new owners decided to tear down all of the building except the relatively solid warehouse section, which had been built in the 1950's.[45] Optimism turns to reality! Today only that modest portion remains and a large amount of used furniture and clothing moves through its doors. Part of the shop yard is used for baseball, softball and touch football, while the old cement pads that were under the sheds and main building await the next passing storm or home run ball. When driving through Starks, an observer should remember there is more to the derelict landscape than meets the eye.

Reuse of Corn Shops

Corn shop buildings varied in size and life expectancy; nevertheless, during their canning years their physical appearance often dominated small villages and neighborhoods in larger communities. They ranged from a few thousand square feet to structures that sometimes exceeded an acre. With closure of the sweet corn business, buildings often stood vacant, fell into decay or were dismantled. In some situations, they were converted to other uses and continue to serve an economic function. Jakle and Wilson present a systematic strategy for understanding the stages of industrial dereliction as manufacturing structures deteriorate: 1. facilities are mothballed but maintained with hope for reopening; 2. facilities are not fully maintained and closure is being delayed; 3. structural abuse to the building occurs as new uses are introduced; 4. abandonment has taken place and there is no maintenance or direct supervision and; 5. demolition is taking place or has been completed.[46]

Forty-seven corn shops or sites where they once stood were visited by me during 1999-2001. Property owners or other knowledgeable people were contacted to determine current use. As with the workers, many shops have passed on. Twenty (43 percent) of the corn factories were entirely gone having succumbed to fire, rot or demolition. A controlled burn of the oldest corn shop, in Farmington, Maine (built in 1868), attracted a fair amount of press coverage (Figure 3.5).[47] Based on an understanding of cannery layouts, the author estimates that 17 (36 percent) remain largely intact (more than half the structure standing) whereas 10 (21%) of the shops had less than half of their structure left (Table 6.24). Without a full tour of every building it's not possible to determine stages of industrial dereliction. However, Jakle and Wilson's five stage framework is helpful for organizing what one observes. None of the shops can be considered stage one or two. A dozen might be considered stage three, but, these usually have some minor portions such as sheds and boiler rooms removed. The remaining portions are often well cared for. I suggest a stage three minus would be useful because in some cases large parts of the building are gone, but what remains is fully used and maintained. Only two canneries clearly fall into stage four, whereas at least twenty-five have been entirely or almost completely removed.

These sites are nearly evenly distributed between small villages (less than 5,000 population), and larger communities (5,000 population or more). In small places, with less economic activity and weaker infrastructure (lack of public water and sewage systems), a high portion of the corn shop locations are now vacant lots. Retail functions, manufacturing and public space are the most frequent uses of buildings or lots they occupied. Structures and lots may have more than one activity; thus, the number of uses is greater than the number of sites visited (Table 6.25). Manufacturing is the most common use, with retail business a close second. Wood products are produced at five of the eleven industrial operations. Other locations involve shoe making, clothing manufacturing, leather tanning and food processing. Two are still canning food, but not sweet corn. Buildings/lots in both small and large communities are used for manufacturing at about the same rate. Retail activities are more common in large towns. These ranged from eating establishments to thrift shops specializing in used clothing and furniture.

Seven sites contained public space- parks, theaters, sewage treatment plants, churches and road right-of-ways. Mixed storage, construction and salvage occupied four sites each. Transportation (trucking) and agriculture (potato farmers) each use two structures. Many of the old shops continue to serve their communities. A number of the buildings that remain have reached a point of deterioration that makes them uneconomical space and strong candidates for removal. In general, those in the larger places have fared better than those in smaller towns.

Time has treated the corn shops the same as it has the workers. Some have passed on leaving a vacant spot, often grassed over. Others are weathered and wrinkled, but still standing, frequently with missing parts. These may continue to serve their communities in some fashion but not to the extent they once did. And, a few are well maintained and full of activity. Thus, if one happens to travel through Northern New England, remember, that corn was packed where now wooden fences are made in Pittsfield, Maine (Figure 6.5); children skate at the James P. Baxter Park and potatoes are prepared for market in Fryeburg, Maine (Figures 6.6 and 6.7); sewage is treated in Fairfield, Maine; Big Mac's and beer are dished out in Farmington, Maine; famous lawn weeds (dandelions), are canned in Wilton, Maine; budget buys on clothing are found in Starks, Maine; auto repair bays are leased in Pittsfield, New Hampshire; and secure storage is available in Randolph, Vermont (Figure 6.8). Like the employees, some can still be encountered but they

N = 47		
	Number	Percent
Greater than half	17	36%
Less than half	10	21%
None	20	43%

Table 6.24   Portion of Corn Shop Building Remaining. *Source:* Author's Survey.

USE	A Small/Big	B Small/Big	C Small/Big	Small/Big = All	
Retail	2/0	1/6	0/1	3/7	= 10
Wholesale	0/1	0/0	0/0	0/1	= 1
Construction/ Salvage	1/0	0/2	1/0	2/2	= 4
Transportation	2/0	0/0	0/0	2/0	= 2
Housing	0/0	1/0	0/1	1/1	= 2
Manufacturing	4/5	0/1	1/0	5/6	= 11
Agriculture	2/0	0/0	0/0	2/0	= 2
Mixed storage space	0/3	0/1	0/0	0/4	= 4
Public space	0/0	2/0	2/4	4/4	= 7
Vacant	0/0	0/0	9/2	9/2	= 11
Total	11/9	4/10	13/8	28/27	= 55

A = Over 50 percent or more of building remains
B = Less than 50 pecent of building remains
C = None of building remains
Big Town   ≥ 5,000 popultaion 24 buildings and lots
Small Town < 5,000 population 23 buildings and lots
Totals may exceed number of corn shops and corn shop lots because
more than one use may take place in a single building or on a single lot.

Table 6.25   Corn Shop Building/Lot Current Use by Size of Town. *Source:* Author's Survey.

Figure 6.5   Fence Factory, Pittsfield, Maine, 2000. *Source*: Author.

Figure 6.6   James P. Baxter Park, Fryeburg, Maine, 2000. *Source*: Author.

Figure 6.7   Potato Operation, Fryeburg, Maine, 2000. *Source*: Author.

Figure 6.8   Secure Storage, Randolph, Vermont, 2000. *Source:* Author.

are not always easy to identify and the number is dwindling. If one wants to see either worker or corn shop, it would be wise to plan a trip before long!

Toponyms

Toponyms, place names, are a cultural imprint on the landscape that often indicate physical attributes and past economic activity. Common in Maine, New Hampshire and Vermont are Mud Pond, Mill Stream, River Road, Town Farm Road, etc. Corn shops have contributed to the eclectic mix of names found on the region's maps. Farmington, Maine, has Corn Shop Lane while Corn Shop Roads appear in Unity and Fryeburg, Maine, (Figure 6.9). Bridgton, Maine, has Corn Shop Brook that used to carry waste water away from the cannery (Figure 6.10). Place names tell much about the past and add a bit of cartographic color. Notwithstanding, even this aspect of the corn canning business is at risk. The good citizens of Monmouth, Maine, saw fit to rename their Corn Shop Road, Lake Shore Drive. Apparently waterfront property owners don't think Corn Shop is high brow enough for their

Figure 6.9   Corn Shop Road, Fryeburg, Maine, 2000. *Source*: Author.

Figure 6.10   Corn Shop Brook, Bridgton, Maine, 2000. *Source*: Author.

desired social standing. Another case of rural gentrification!

   Passage of elderly people and obsolete buildings, despite their contributions to communities, is expected. Purging the cultural landscape of names associated with symbols of economic pride may be carrying toponym sanitization too far. If residents along a corn shop road erase their linkage to canning gold, there is a possibility that entire communities may do the same. To understand the present, evidence of the past needs to be retained. This is a struggle not only for corn shop towns but any place confronting economic and social change.

Chapter 7

Summary and Observations

A grain mutant turns into a popular vegetable. Northern New England, a place with limited agricultural options, has a physical environment that is an excellent match to the mutant's needs. Seamen, tinsmiths and farmers figure out how to grow, process and market a healthy treat with a long shelf life. Demands of war, westward migrations and urbanization created strong markets which stimulated farm and factory innovations. An industry was born that bonded farmers, factory workers and owners for the good of the entire community. Income was earned by many, with fortunes made by some. Another war with its government contracts and expanding civilian consumption pushed the business to dizzy heights only to be followed by depression and contraction.

In addition to global economic conditions, competition from other places took its toll on the region's corn shops. Then another war and new government contracts to be filled saved the day for the remaining producers. With peace in 1945, corn packing in Maine, New Hampshire and Vermont began its long final slide ending in 1968. The demise was driven by competition, new technology that was more advantageous to producers outside the area, and changing agricultural economics in Northern New England.

Crop, canneries and people combined to shape aspects of the region's landscape. In some localities sweet corn was the primary cash crop with thousands of acres planted. At least 136 towns had corn shops with some having several. At harvest time, canners of gold would appear by the thousands to process the tons of corn arriving from the fields in horse drawn carts, tractor-pulled wagons, and trucks.

Working together as a team were governors, millionaires, future lawyers and professors, farmers, farm wives, housewives, woodsmen, carpenters, African-Americans, Canadians, German POW's and their guards, war veterans, children and others. Corn shop closure was the beginning of the end of community in many small towns. It takes a few generations for the process to run its course. During canning season, nearly every family had at least one member involved in picking or packing. Today there may be as many or more people in the towns, but they are commuting (tele or in body) to dispersed employment opportunities. Few can imagine joining their neighbors for six weeks in late summer and fall to can corn. There was little evidence of a social class structure in the corn shops and everyone had a role to play. The sweet corn industry was imbedded in the larger global system and responded to both positive and negative events. The business grew, had a good run and then disappeared as internal and external forces shaped its fortunes. A parade of world characters passed through the enterprise; Nazi officers to a United State's Senator (Bert Fernald). The local corn factory appears to have been an excellent barometer for tracking globalization.

Commercial activities that survive for long periods in an ever changing world must adapt to innovates and markets. Sweet corn canning in Northern New England was not able to withstand the global dynamics of post-World War Two. Environmental and economic constraints limited options. More organized promotion of the region's reputation for high quality sweet corn and factory consolidation to gain economy of scale might have slowed the decline and even saved some shops. Fragmented marketing, decentralized leadership and small undercapitalized operations inhibited sustainability.

With the departure of the industry, former sweet corn acreage went into other uses (hay, field corn, forests, housing subdivisions, etc). Farmers, owners and workers explored new ways of generating income but continue to recall the impact canning gold had on their lives. Corn shops deteriorated and many disappeared over time. Some were renovated for other uses, not unlike a former worker finding another job. Over time both people and corn shops pass from the landscape. The buildings that remain have been transformed into structures that do not suggest they were corn shops. For years to come, an occasional obituary will include a comment about the departed having worked in a corn factory. A few road names will continue to proclaim the location of a shop.

During the past half century, I watched this story unfold and recognized that much of it is part of my life. I experienced the wonder of harvesting a near-perfect field of sweet corn and hauling the crop to the shop where I followed its conversion into cans of gold. The sounds, smells, work ethic and social atmosphere of the canneries are forever etched into my mind. Sadness, due to the local shop's demise, remains with me. I watched the old factory near my childhood home and the people that worked there slowly fad away. Every time another section is taken down (only a small portion remains), and with each death of a former worker (there are still a fair number left), I lose a bit of my tangible heritage. The process is gradual, much like landscape change.

Industries pass through stages as they originate, mature and decline. Landsacpe change is part of industrial evolution. Relics of the past activity remain after closure. These are less noticable over time as they are removed or retrofitted for other uses. As people that were part of the industry pass on, interest in what happened declines. The rate at which old factories disappear and memories fade varies. A significant benchmark in this process is the passing of those that worked in the business. This research was done close to that point in time. I encourage anyone considering a study of change to begin before the principals involved go to their final rest. They are the richest resource for understanding change. More work needs to be done on the pace of disappearance, but change will not stop while plans are being made.

Occasionally, I have sensed Carl Sauer watching over my shoulder. From time to time, I've tried to think of quesions he might raise and have attempted to address them. He was keen about landscape and valued the ability of local people in understanding process. I suspect he would see the recent globalization bandwagon as basic geography.

Sweet corn canning is one of the forces that shaped the character of rural Northern New England. Every locale has its own set of landscape dynamics. I hope this work enhances one's understanding of how a specific enterprise contributes to a region's evolution.

Time Warp

What does the future hold for other industries, people and places? Progress is often a frightening experience. Frequently the things that one understands best are most noticeable when they disappear. Questions arise about the future of other landscapes that have been partly formed by an individual commodity- cattle in the American West, rice in California or cheese in Wisconsin.

There are also opportunities to apply this understanding of economic and cultural landscape change to developing regions of the world. In August 2000, my wife Liz and I happened to be venturing along the most famous road named in honor of an agricultural commodity, the Silk Road, in the northwestern China Province of Xinjiang. The route was dotted with long abandoned towns that fell into decline when transportation technology of the 1400's and 1500's made it possible to by-pass the region with sea passage from Europe to China. Some communities with extensive oasis farming continued to exist and even prosper as producers of food items for export.

Canning season had arrived and as we passed through a tomato growing region in the Tarim Basin and entered a cannery town, a traffic jam appeared, not an uncommon event in a country with 1.25 billion people. Truck and tractor-pulled carts laden with tomatoes stretched for more than a mile, a back-up caused by mechanical problems in the canning factory. The odors of tomatoes, grease and oil from the farm equipment, and cigarette smoke hung heavily in the hot afternoon air. The breakdown had caused a long delay and it was evident that the haulers at the front were running out of patience while others were just arriving at the rear. Many conversations were underway among the men involved, but the big concern had to be the decline in fruit quality with each additional hour it stayed in the truck or wagon. Change the crop to sweet corn, the language to English and this could be a scene from a Northern New England corn shop town half a century earlier. Is it possible to go back to the past? On the other hand, can a Chinese farmer see the future by visiting Corn Shop Road, Fryeburg, Maine? The latter may be the more telling question. Both address globalization and the rate of regional change.

Knowledge of the past is critical to understanding present patterns and anticipating future geographies. I hopes this book will make each reader more aware of historical geography, supply answers about landscape change and raise questions about the future. Enjoy your next can of gold, probably from some flat, fertile place in Minnesota.

Appendices

APPENDIX A

STATIONS UTILIZED FOR MOISTURE INDEX
AND POTENTIAL EVAPOTRANSPIRATION[a]

Location of Canneries Processing Sweet Corn in 1967[b]	Station	PE	MI
Frederick, Maryland	Same	751	37
Rochester, Minnesota	Same	614	20
Red Lodge, Montana	Same	496	2
Reinbeck, Iowa	Waterloo, Iowa	607	18
Rossville, Illinois	Urbana, Illinois	691	30
Neward, New York	Rochester, N.Y.	638	31
Sauk City, Wisconsin	Madison, Wisconsin	647	20
St. Georges, Delaware	Milford, Delaware	733	43
New Freedom, Penn.	Harrisburg, Penn.	722	32
St. Marys, Ohio	Lima, Ohio	678	39
Emmett, Idaho	Same	701	-60
Cowley, Wyoming	Powell, Wyoming	578	-74
Walla Walla, Washington	Same	749	-44
Freedom, Maine	Bangor, Maine	651	49
Belvedere, Illinois	Rockford, Illinois	692	27
Fowler, Indiana	Lafayette, Indiana	705	40
Silverton, Oregon	Portland, Oregon	706	52
Green Bay, Wisconsin	Same	610	18
Cokato, Minnesota	St. Cloud, Minn.	622	8
Provo, Utah	Same	640	-40

Abandoned Canneries	Station	PE	MI
Portland, Maine	Same	593	80
Rumford, Maine	Same	571	73
Essex Junction, Vt.	Burlington, Vt.	621	33
Pittsfield, N.H.	Concord, N.H.	606	61
Randolph, Vt.	Northfield, Vt.	548	52

Sites in American Corn Belt	Station	PE	MI
Effingham, Illinois	Same	763	29
Davenport, Iowa	Same	698	19
Lincoln, Illinois	Same	720	15
Springfield, Illinois	Same	747	21
South Bend, Indiana	Same	680	31
Lincoln, Nebraska	Same	742	- 6
Ames, Iowa	Same	679	14
Grand Island, Nebraska	Same	723	-13
Des Moines, Iowa	Same	710	9
Chillicothe, Missouri	Same	764	39
Dayton, Ohio	Same	727	29
Mount Ayr, Ohio	Same	694	28
Aurora, Illinois	Same	657	35
Mount Vermont, Illinois	Same	791	31
Terre Haute, Indiana	Same	768	32

Antiquity Sites	Station	PE	MI
Jalisco (State), Mexico	Guadalajara, Mexico	876	7
Jemez Cave, New Mexico	Jemez Springs, N.M.	639	-30
Aztec Ruins, New Mexico	Aztec, New Mexico	660	-65

[a] Data from a nearby weather station are used in cases where cannery towns or antiquity sites do not have facilities to supply climatic information. There may be a slight degree of variation in micro-climate between cannery towns/sites and weather stations.

[b] National Canners Association, *Canners Directory 1967-1968* (Washington, D.C.: National Canners Association, 1967), pp. 166-167.

APPENDIX B

VALUE OF ALL COMMERCIAL VEGETABLES FOR PROCESSING
(Thousands of Dollars)

	1930	1940	1950	1960	1965
Maine	$ 1,594	$ 831	$ 1,646	$ 1,642	$ 1,669
New Hampshire	74	17	81	a	a
Vermont	111	41	63	a	a
Delaware	1,361	1,213	4,418	5,760	7,229
Idaho	a	140	1,463	3,136	4,581
Illinois	3,250	2,808	9,050	14,709	17,084
Indiana	7,369	5,437	6,764	a	a
Iowa	1,841	907	1,496	1,351	1,275
Maryland	2,895	4,897	10,728	9,737	12,668
Michigan	2,675	2,293	6,840	a	a
Minnesota	2,454	2,831	7,820	9,791	16,320
Nebraska	142	82	70	a	a
New York	5,871	4,682	15,642	16,696	16,858
Ohio	2,003	1,975	4,662	a	a
Oregon	a	2,022	12,901	18,219	25,853
Pennsylvania	644	2,574	7,811	7,942	7,520
Tennessee	805	a	a	a	a
Utah	a	1,526	3,139	a	a
Virginia	a	1,904	4,030	a	a
Washington	a	2,035	10,216	16,894	26,768
Wisconsin	9,641	6,774	18,934	19,619	35,318
Other States	27	44,989	78,858	16,665	232,801
United States	70,856	68,799	206,632	287,161	405,944

a Included in other states

Source: U.S.D.A. *Commercial Vegetables,* 1953, 18-22; *Vegetables for Processing,* 1967, Table 2.

Notes

Chapter 1

Introduction

1. Carl O. Sauer established the department of geography at the University of California and is considered the most influential cultural geographer on the mid-twentieth century.

2. Works that are representative of Sauer's interest in plant origins and include discussions of the role of corn (maize) in early agriculture include Carl O. Sauer, "American Agricultural Origins: A Consideration of Nature and Culture" in *Essays in Anthropology Presented to A. L. Kroeber in Celebration of His Sixtieth Birthday June 11, 1936* (Berkeley, Calif.: University of California Press, 1936), 279-297; "Theme of Plant and Animal Destruction in Economic History," *Journal of Farm Economics* 20 (1938): 765-775; *Agricultural Origins and Dispersals: The Domestication of Animals and Foodstuffs* (Boston: Massachusetts Institute of Technology Press, 1952).

3. Paul B. Frederic, "Historical Geography of the Northern New England Sweet Corn Canning Industry" (master's thesis, Southern Illinois University, 1968a).

4. Papers presented over the years include Paul B. Frederic "Historical Geography of the Northern New England Sweet Corn Canning Industry" (at meeting of the West Lakes Division of the Association of American Geographers, Madison, Wis., 18 October 1968b); "Pre-Canning Antiquity of Sweet Corn" (at meeting of the Illinois Academy of Science, Decatur, Ill., fall 1969); "Rural Industrial Development: The Case of Vegetable Canneries in Maine" (at meeting of Eastern Historical Geographers Association, Geneseo, N.Y. 24 September 1983); "Canners of Gold: Northern New England Corn Shop

Workers 1860-1968" (at meeting of Eastern Historical Geographers Association, Bar Harbor, Maine, 21 October 2000); "The Northern New England Sweet Corn Canning Industry and its Demise" (at meeting of the New England-St. Lawrence Valley Geographical Society, Providence, R.I., 29 October 2000); "Former Vegetable Canneries in Northern New England: Resource or Blight?" (at meeting of the Association of American Geographers, New York, N.Y., 1 March 2001).

    5. For overviews of research approaches in agricultural geography see Howard F. Gregor, *Geography of Agriculture: Themes in Research* (Englewood Cliffs, N.J.: Prentice Hall, Inc., 1970); C. Morris and N. J. Evens, "Research on the Geography of Agricultural Change: Redundant or Revitalized?" *Area* 31 (1999), 349-358.

    6. Joseph E. Spencer and Ronald J. Horvath, "How Does an Agricultural Region Originate?" *Annals of the Association of American Geographers* 53 (1963): 79-92, discuss the role of these six cultural processes in shaping agricultural regions..

    7. Loyal Durand, Jr., "Cheese Region of Southeastern Wisconsin," *Economic Geography* 15 (1939): 283-292; "Cheese Region of Northwestern Illinois," *Economic Geography* 22 (1946): 24-37; Gordon R. Lewthwaite, "Wisconsin Cheese and Farm Type: A Locational Hypothesis," *Economic Geography* 40 (1947): 95-112, examine the role of a manufactured dairy product in shaping the character of a region; Mary Beth Pudup and Michael J. Watts, "Growing Against the Grain: Mechanized Rice Farming in the Sacramento Valley, California" in B. L. Turner, and S. B. Brush, eds., *Comparative Farming Systems* (New York: Guilford Press, 1987), 345-384, explore how mechanical devices transform an agricultural landscape; Paul F. Starrs, *Let The Cowboy Ride: Cattle Ranching in the American West* (Baltimore: Johns Hopkins Press, 1998), gallops across the range and writes of its change.

    8. Michael Troughton, "From Nodes to Nodes: The Rise and Fall of Agricultural Activity in the Maritimes" in Douglas Day, ed. *Geographical Perspectives on the Maritime Provinces* (Halifax: St. Mary's University Press, 1988), 25-46, examines a large complex region; John Fraser Hart, "Land Use Change in a Piedmont County," *Annals of the Association of American Geographers* 70 (1980): 492-525, tackles the details of change in a single county.

    9. Michael Bunce and Gerald Walker, "The Transformation of Rural Life: The Case of Toronto's Countryside," in Ian Bowler, Christopher R. Bryant and M. Duane Nellis, eds. *Contemporary Rural Systems in*

Transition: Economy and Society, Volume Two (London: CAB International, 1992), 49-61, focus on urban encroachment into rural space; John Hudson, *Plains Country Towns* (Minneapolis: University of Minnesota Press, 1985); Thomas L. Daniels and Mark Lapping "Small Town Triage: A Rural Settlement Policy for the American Midwest," *Journal of Rural Studies* 3 (1987): 273-280, document changing fortunes of small towns in the U.S. heartland; Marty Strange, *Family Farming: A New Economic View* (Lincoln, Neb.: University of Nebraska Press, 1988), presents farmers' perspectives; Brian Ilbery and Ian Bowler, "From Agricultural Productivism to Post-productivism" in Brian Ilbery, ed., *The Geography of Rural Change* (London: Longman, 1998), 57-85, evaluate some implications of the post-production countryside.

10. Carl O. Sauer, "The Morphology of Landscape," *University of California Publications in Geography* 2 (1925), 19-54.

11. Collectively, the following provide an excellent sweep of rural America's landscape and its meanings. John A. Jakle and David Wilson, *Derelict Landscapes: The Wasting of America's Built Environment* (Savage, Md.: Rowman and Littlefield Publishers, 1992); Wilber Zelinsky, *Exploring the Beloved Country: Geographical Forays into American Society and Culture* (Iowa City, Iowa: University of Iowa Press, 1994); George Thompson, ed. *Landscape in America* (Austin Tex.: University of Texas Press, 1995); Paul Groth and Todd W. Bressi, *Understanding Ordinary Landscapes* (New Haven, Conn.: Yale University Press, 1997); John Fraser Hart, *The Rural Landscape* (Baltimore: John Hopkins Press, 1998).

12. Positive and negative aspects of globalization are discussed by Glen Norcliffe, "Canada in a Global Economy," *Canadian Geographer* 45 (2001):14; Michael Storper, "The Limits to Globalization: Technology Districts and International Trade," *Economic Geography* 68 (1992): 60-93.

13. For review of spatial diffusion and disappearance see Lawrence A. Brown, *Innovation Diffusion: A New Pespective* (New York: Methuen, 1981); Paul B. Frederic, "An Analysis of Spatial Disappearance: The Case of Dairying in a Cash Grain Region," (Ph.D. dissertation, University of Illinois, 1973).

14. John Steinbeck, *Cannery Row* (New York: Viking Press, 1945); Tom Mangelsdorf, *A History of Steinbeck's Cannery Row* (Santa Cruz, Calif.: Western Tanager Press, 1986); Michael K. Hemp, *Official Cannery Row Visitor's Guide: A Shopping, Dining and Activities Guide*

to John Steinbeck's Historic Cannery Row (Monterey, Calif.: Cannery Row Company, 1998).

CHAPTER 2

Pre-Canning Antiquity of Sweet Corn

1. George F. Carter, "Sweet Corn Among the Indians," *Geographical Review* 38 (1998): 206.
2. Paul C. Mangelsdorf, "The Origin of Corn," *Scientific America* 255 (1986): 85-86.
3. Paul C. Mangelsdorf, *Corn: Its Origin, Evolution and Improvement* (Cambridge, Mass.: Belknap Press of Harvard University, 1974), 107-109.
4. A. T. Erwin, "Sweet Corn - Its Origin and Importance as an Indian Food Plant in the United States," *Iowa State College Journal of Science* 8 (1934): 389.
5. J. T. Gerdes and W. F. Tracy, "Diversity of Historically Important Sweet Corn Imbreds as Estimated by RFLPs, Morphology Isozymes and Pedigree," *Crop Science* 34 (1994).
6. Walter A. Huelsen, *Sweet Corn* (New York, N.Y.: Interscience Publishers, 1954), 12-13.
7. Alphonse De Candolle, *Origin of Cultivated Plants* (New York: Hafner Publishing Company, 1886), 395.
8. Erwin, "Sweet Corn - Its Origin," 388.
9. H. G. Alexander and Paul Reiter, *Report on the Excavation of Jemez Cave, New Mexico* University of New Mexico Bulletin 278 (Albuquerque, N. Mex.: University of New Mexico Press, 1935), 62; E. F. Castetter and W. H. Bell, "Pima and Papago Indian Agriculture" in *Inter-American Studies, One* (Albuquerque, N. Mex.: University of New Mexico Press, 1942), 86.
10. G. W. Hendry, "Archeological Evidence Concerning the Origin of Sweet Maize," *Journal of the Society of American Agronomy* 22 (1930): 513.
11. Erwin, "Sweet Corn - Its Origin," 388.
12. Carl O. Sauer, *Agricultural Origins and Dispersals: The Domestication of Animals and Foodstuffs* (Boston: Massachusetts Institute of Technology Press, 1952), 65-72.
13. Sissel Johannessen and Christine A. Hastorf, "Corn and Culture

in Central Andean Prehistory," *Science* 244 (1989): 692.

14. E. J. Wellhausen, L. M. Roberts and E. Hernandez X, *Races of Maize in Mexico* (Cambridge, Mass.: Bessy Institute of Harvard, 1952), 80.

15. A. T. Erwin, "Sweet Corn Not An Important Indian Food Plant in the Pre-Columbian Period," *Journal of The American Society of Agronomy* 39 (1947): 118.

16. Isabel Kelley and Edgar Anderson, "Sweet Corn in Jalisco," *Annals of the Missouri Botanical Garden* 30 (1943): 409-410.

17. Irwin, "Sweet Corn - Its Origin," 386.

18. George F. Will and George E. Hyde, *Corn Among the Indians of the Upper Missouri* (Lincoln, Nebr.: University of Nebraska Press, 1917), 117.

19. John Witthoft, *Green Corn Ceremonialism in The Eastern Woodlands* (Ann Arbor, Mich.: University of Michigan Press, 1949), 32.

20. G. Carter, "Sweet Corn Among," 208; P. Mangelsdorf, *Corn: Its Origin,* p. 110, both note evidence supporting the introduction of Iroquois sweet corn into New England from the western region of New York by returning members of General Sullivan's expedition against the Six Nations in 1779.

21. Will and Hyde, *Corn Among,* 299-317.

22. Irwin, "Sweet Corn - Its Origin," 389.

23. A. T. Irwin. "Anent The Origin of Sweet Corn," *Iowa State College Journal of Science* 16(1942): 485.

24. G. Carter, "Sweet Corn Among," 208.

25. A. T. Erwin, "Sweet Corn - Mutant or Historic Species?" *Economic Botany* 30 (1951): 302.

26. Ibid., 303.

27. Irwin, "Anent the Origin," 485.

28. Irwin, "Sweet Corn - Its Origin," 387.

CHAPTER 3

Birth of The Industry, 1840-1879

1. J. G. Mosier, title unknown, Agricultural Experiment Station Bulletin 208 (Urbana, Ill.: University of Illinois, 1918).

2. Walter A. Huelsen, *Sweet Corn* (New York: Interscience

Publishers, 1954), 234.

3.   Ibid., 241.

4.   Douglas B. Carter, "Modern Climatic Classification: Competition or Evolution," *Publications in Climatology* 19 (1966), 310.

5.   Ibid., 321.

6.   Ibid., 323.

7.   Victor R. Boswell, "Vegetables," *Yearbook of Agriculture: Soil* (Washington, D.C.: United States Department of Agriculture, 1957), 697.

8.   Albert S. Carlson and John Weston, "The Sweet Corn Industry in Maine," *Economic Geography* 10 (1934): 393.

9.   Ibid., 391.

10. C. A. Magoon and C. W. Culpepper, "The Relation of Seasonal Factors to Quality of Sweet Corn," *Journal of Agricultural Research* 33 (1926): 1071-1072.

11. N. C. Brady, R. A. Struchtemeyer and R. B. Musgrave, "The Northeast," *Yearbook of Agriculture: Soil* (Washington, D.C.: United States Department of Agriculture, 1957), 601.

12. John A. Ferwerda et al., *The Soils of Maine* Maine Agricultural and Forest Experiment Station Miscellaneous Report 402 (Orono, Maine: University of Maine, 1997), 13.

13. Henry A. Wallace and Earl N. Bressman, *Corn and Corn Growing* (New York, N.Y.: John Wiley and Sons, 1928), 160.

14. E. S. Judge, "American Canning Interests" in Chancey M. De Pew, ed., *One Hundred Years of American Commerce* (New York: D. O. Hayes and Company, 1895), 396.

15. Lucine H. Lombard, "How A Big Industry Started Near Portland," *Portland (Maine) Sunday Telegram* 20 October 1907.

16. Chester C. Soule, "The Growth of the Corn Canning Industry," 1909 paper in the files of the Monmouth Canning Company, collection of Peter Soule, Union, Maine.

17. Bert M. Fernald, "Maine Canning Industry" in *Three Able Addresses Delivered Before the State Board of Trade at Bangor, Maine March 25, 1902* (Portland, Maine: Marks Printing House, 1902), 4.

18. Ibid., 5.

19. C. Soule, "The Growth of the Corn."

20. N. Winslow and Company, "Early Corn Canning," 1888 paper in Winslow Collection, Maine Historical Society Library, Portland Maine.

21. Joyce Bibber, "Nearly All in the Family: Nathan Winslow and His Family Network," *Maine Historical Society Quarterly* 28 (1989): 202.

22. Lombard, "How a Big Industry."

23. Bibber, "Nearly All in the Family."

24. Earl May, *The Canning Clan* (New York: Macmillan Company, 1937), 19.

25. Clarence A Day, *Farming in Maine: 1860-1940* (Orono, Maine: University of Maine Press, 1963), 29.

26. William E. S. Whitman, *The Wealth and Industry of Maine, First Annual Report* (Augusta, Maine: Unknown publisher, 1873), 18.

27. Ibid., 326.

28. Marshall Edwards, former Superintendent of the Monmouth Canning Company shop in Starks, Maine. The author visited him many times during the past few years and he was a wonderful source of information about the corn canning business. He passed away 22 February 2000. Interview by author, Farmington, Maine 7 January 2000.

29. W. Lyman Underwood, "Incidents in the Canning Industry of New England," in Arthur J. Judge, ed., *A History of the Canning Industry by its Most Prominent Men* (Baltimore: National Canners and Allied Associations, 1914), 13.

30. Huelsen, *Sweet Corn*, 271.

31. Day, *Farming in Maine*, 29.

32. Huelsen, *Sweet Corn,* 260-261.

33. James P. Baxter, "A Brief History of the Canning Industry in Maine," *First Biennial Report of the Commission of Sea and Shore Fisheries of the State of Maine* (Auburn, Maine: Merrill and Webber Company, 1919), 5.

34. *Maine Farmer*, 14 November 1868.

35. Huelsen, *Sweet Corn*, 261.

36. Ibid., 264.

37. Ibid., 261.

38. Karl Sax, *Sweet Corn Breeding Experiments* Agricultural Experiment Station Bulletin 332 (Orono, Maine: University of Maine, 1926), 115.

39. V. P. Hedrick, *A History of Horticulture in America to 1860* (New York: Oxford University Press, 1950), 461.

40. Ibid., 462.

41. A. T. Irwin, "Sweet Corn - Mutant or Historic Species?" *Economic Botany* 30 (1951): 305.

42. Huelsen, *Sweet Corn*, 51.

43. Percy Wells Bidwell and John J. Falconer, *History of Agriculture in Northern United States* (New York: Peter Smith, 1941), 300-301.

44. *Maine Farmer*, 14 November 1868.

45. S. S. Smith, "The Growing of Sweet Corn for Canning," in *Twenty-fifth Annual Report of Maine Board of Agriculture* (Augusta, Maine: Sprage and Son, 1881), 122-123.

46. Former corn shop worker (1930's - 1960's) who wished to remain anonymous concerning comments that might be offensive to people who were once employed in the canneries. Interview by author, Farmington, Maine, 6 March 2000.

47. Elspeth Brown, "Gender and Identity in Rural Maine Women and the *Maine Farmer*, 1870-1875" *Maine Historical Society Quarterly* 33 (1993), provides helpful comments on rural women and wage labor during the 1870's.

48. Martin Brown, Jens Christiansen and Peter Philips, "The Decline of Child Labor in the U.S. Fruit and Vegetable Canning Industry: Law or Economics," *Business History Review* 66 (1992).

49. Huelsen, *Sweet Corn*, 275.

50. Neil Rolde, *The Baxters of Maine: Downeast Visionaries* (Gardiner, Maine: Tilbury House Publishers, 1997).

CHAPTER 4

Growth and Development of The Industry, 1880 - 1930

1.   Clarence A. Day, *Farming in Maine: 1860-1940* (Orono, Maine: University of Maine Press, 1963), 27.

2.   Russell Bailey, Head of Plant Breeding Program, University of Maine Experimental Station. Interview by author. Monmouth, Maine 16 June 1967. Excerpt in Paul B. Frederic, "Historical Geography of the Northern New England Sweet Corn Canning Industry," (master's thesis Southern Illinois University, 1968), 59-60.   Mr. Bailey also shared his personal collection of sweet corn papers.

3. John Donald Black, *The Rural Economy of New England* (Cambridge, Mass.: Harvard University Press, 1950), 530-531.

4. *Maine Farmer*, 12 January 1882.

5. *Maine Farmer*, 16 January 1882.

6. *Maine Farmer*, 22 June 1882.

7. James Berry Vickery III, *A History of the Town of Unity, Maine* (Manchester, Maine: Falmouth Publishing House, 1954), 143.

8. Harold Fisher Wilson, "The Roads of Windsor," *Geographical Review* 21 (1931): 390.

9. Samuel T. Pickard, "Portland" in Lyman P. Powell, ed. *Historic Towns of New England* (New York: G. P. Putnam's Sons, 1899), 64-65.

10. Karl Soule, President of Monmouth Canning Company. Interviewed by author, Portland, Maine 16 June 1967. Excerpt in Paul B. Frederic, "Historical Geography of the Northern New England Sweet Corn Canning Industry," (master's thesis Southern Illinois University, 1968), 68-69.

11. T. L. S. Morse, "Black and Gay Marks Half Century of Canning," *Rockland (Maine) Courier Gazette* 16 November 1961.

12. Nellie Frederic, scrapbook 1925 - 1945 in collection of Madge Frederic, Starks, Maine.

13. *Skowhegan (Maine) Independent Reporter* unknown day September 1916.

14. K. Soule, President.

15. John W. Gault, Secretary of the Maine Canners and Freezers Association letter to F. Webster Browne 2 May 1962.

16. Commissioner of Agriculture, *Agriculture of Maine* (Augusta, Maine: State of Maine, 1919), 138.

17. Day, *Farming in Maine*, 33-35.

18. James W. Lanigan, Minutes of the Maine Canners Association, 17 December 1919, 93.

19. Ibid., 28 June 1921, 110.

20. Ibid., 29 March 1922, 125.

21. Day, *Farming in Maine*, 34.

22. Commissioner of Agriculture, *Agriculture of Maine, 1922-1924* (Augusta, Maine: State of Maine, 1924), 11.

23. Adrian Wells Sr., Owner of W. S. Wells Canning Company. Interview by author, Wilton, Maine 9 February 2000.

24. Norman Elliott, Superintendent of canning factory in Freedom, Maine. He managed the plant under the ownership of Monmouth

Canning Company, continued after it was sold to A. L. Stewart in the mid-1960's, and oversaw its closure. Notes provided to author 1967. Additional comments are found in Paul B. Frederic, "Historical Geography of the Northern New England Sweet Corn Canning Industry" (master's thesis Southern Illinois University, 1968), 76-77.

25. McIntire-Sawin, Camp records, 15 August 1912, Waterford, Maine.

26. Huelsen, *Sweet Corn*, 268.

27. Earl May, *The Canning Clan* (New York, N.Y.: Macmillan Company, 1937), 132-133.

28. James H. Collins, *The Story of Canned Foods* (New York, N.Y: E. P. Dutton and Company, 1924), 70-71.

29. Huelsen, *Sweet Corn*, 272.

30. Frank W. Smith, *Apparatus For Treating or Sterilizing Canned Food, Patent Number 664,642* (Washington, D.C.: United States Patent Office, 1898).

31. John Jennings, *Apparatus for Steaming and Processing Canned Goods, Patent Number 740,981* (Washington, D.C.: United States Patent Office, 1903); Ralph B. Polk, *Apparatus for Treating Canned Goods, Patent Number 742,488* (Washington, D.C.: United States Patent Office, 1903).

32. Henry L. Forhan, *Revolver for Processing Canned Goods, Patent Number 900,064* (Washington, D.C.: United States Patent Office, 1908).

33. May, *The Canning Clan*, 263-265.

34. Jewett Collection includes extensive material on the multi-generation family canning business in Somerset County, Maine. The G. S. and F. E. Jewett Company operated from 1910 to the 1950's. Involvement of individuals is diagramed in the family tree item 1532, Maine Historical Society Library, Portland, Maine.

35. May, *The Canning Clan*, 359-360.

36. Huelsen, *Sweet Corn*, 50.

37. May, *The Canning Clan*, 46-47.

38. Ibid., 50-52.

39. Miles E. Langley, Representative of the Portland Packing Company. Letter to W. E. Elwell, 22 November 1924.

40. Huelsen, 52-55.

41. Byron D. Halsted, ed. *Barns, Sheds and Outbuildings: Placement, Design and Construction* 1881; reprint, Brattleboro, Vt.:

Stephen Green Press, 1980), 210-223, is an example of silo promotional literature of the late 1800's; Allen G. Noble and Richard K. Cleek, *The Old Barns Book: A Guide to North American Barns and Other Farm Structures* (New Brunswick, N.J.: Rutgers University Press, 1995), 157-161, review silo types.

42. N. Frederic, scrapbook 1925 - 1945.

43. For a discussion of agricultural land use and transportation models see P. Hall, ed. *von Thunen's Isolated State,* trans. Carla M. Watenberg (Oxford: Pergamon, 1966); Howard F. Gregor, *Geography of Agriculture: Themes in Research* (Englewood Cliffs, N.J.: Prentice-Hall, 1970), 57-71; W. B. Morgan and R. J. C. Munton, *Agricultural Geography* (New York: St. Martin's Press, 1971), 70-88.

44. *Progress of Agricultural Experiments* Agricultural Experiment Station Bulletin 221 (Durham, N.H.: University of New Hampshire, 1924), 12.

45. For reviews of the struggle to adjust to agricultural and social change see Richard H. Condon, "Living in Two Worlds: Rural Maine in 1930," *Maine Historical Society Quarterly* 25 (1985): 57-58; Thomas C. Hubka, *Big House, Little House, Back House Barn: The Connecting Farm Buildings of New England* (Hanover, N.H.: University Press of New England, 1984).

46. Burton Sanderson, Diary for years 1890 - 1900 in collection of David Sanderson, Waterford, Maine.

47. Ephrain Jillson, son of corn shop owner George Jillson. Interview by author, Otisfield, Maine, 12 March 2000.

48. *Bureau of Industrial and Labor Statistics for the State of Maine Fourteenth Annual Report, 1900* (Augusta, Maine: *Kennebec Journal,* 1901), 72; John M. Winslow, "Our Canning Interests," *Agriculture of Maine, Forty-fourth Annual Report* (Augusta, Maine: State of Maine, 1901), 198.

49. S. S. Smith, "The Growing of Sweet Corn For Canning," in *Twenty-fifth Annual Report of Maine Board of Agriculture* (Augusta, Maine: Sprage and Son, 1881), 121.

50. Martin Brown, Jens Christiansen, and Peter Philips, "The Decline of Child Labor in the U.S. Fruit and Vegetable Industry: Law or Economics?" *Business History Review* 66 (1992): 768-770.

51. Jillson.

52. Jane E. Radcliffe, "Perspectives on Children in Maine's Canning Industry, 1907-1911," *Maine Historical Society Quarterly* 24 (1985).

53. "Burnham & Morrill, Labor Roster for Strong, Maine Cannery 16 September 1917" in collection of Richard Gold, Farmington, Maine, with permission of B & M Division of B & G Foods.

54. Arthur Hill began work in corn canneries during World War One and continued to be employed in the industry until the 1960's. Mr. Hill passed away soon after his conversation with the author. Interview by author, Fryeburg, Maine, 21 March 2000.

55. Burnham & Morrill, "Time Sheet for Strong Cannery," 1920 (probably), in collection of Richard Gould, Farmington, Maine, with permission of B & M Division of B & G Foods.

56. Burnham & Morrill, "Pay Statement for Rose Kennedy," 1 October 1920 (probably), in collection of Richard Gold, Farmington, Maine, with permission of B & M Division of B & G Foods.

57. Burnham & Morrill, "Labor Roster;" Burnham & Morrill, "List of Farmers Contracting to Plant Corn for Strong Cannery, 1926," in collection of Richard Gould, Farmington, Maine with permission of B & M Division of B and G Foods.

58. Burnham & Morrill, "List of Farmers Contracting."

59. John W. Gault address delivered before the Maine Canners and Freezers Association, 11 February 1958.

60. Harold Fisher Wilson, *The Hill Country of Northern New England* (New York: Morningside Heights Columbia University Press, 1936), 137.

61 May, *The Canning Clan*, 48-49.

62. Bert M. Fernald, "Maine Canning Industry" in *Three Able Addresses Delivered Before the State Board of Trade at Bangor, Maine March 25, 1902* (Portland, Maine: Marks Printing House, 1902), 7-8.

63. L. V. Burton, "Corn Shops Down in Maine, Part Two," *Food Industries* 3 (February 1936): 64.

CHAPTER 5

Decline of The Industry, 1931 - 1968

1. John Donald Black, The *Rural Economy of New England* (Cambridge, Mass.: Harvard University Press, 1950), 531-532.

2. Norman Elliott, See Chapter 4, note 24.

3. Frank. P. Washburn, *Agriculture of Maine: Twenty-Ninth Report of the Commissioner of Agriculture of the State of Maine* (Augusta,

Maine: State of Maine, 1940), 39.

4. Clarence A. Day., *Farming in Maine: 1860-1940* (Orono, Maine: University of Maine, 1963), 282-283.

5. Richard Gould owned the Franklin Farms Products Company's cannery in Farmington, Maine, and managed it for two decades. Mr. Gould has offered much welcome advice to the author. Interview by author, Farmington, Maine, 7 March 2000.

6. Charles S. Morrill, *B & M: What Two Young Maine Men Founded Eighty Years Ago* (New York: Newcomer Society of North America, 1950), 15.

7. Compiled by author. See sources for Figure 1.1.

8. Karl Soule, 1967. See Chapter 4, note 10.

9. Harold Harmon, President of H. S. Forham Company. Interview by author, Portland, Maine, 6 June 1967. Excerpt in Paul B. Frederic, "Historical Geography of the Northern New England Sweet Corn Canning Industry" (master's thesis Southern Illinois University, 1969), 105.

10. Frank O. Brown, former fire chief and road crew foreman (New Sharon, Maine), who also worked in local corn shops. Interview by author, New Sharon, Maine, 18 February 2000.

11. Ina Porter Turner, "Corn Canning in Maine" interview by Naomi Schalit, Maine Public Broadcasting Corporation, 26 June 2000.

12. K. Soule, 1967. See Chapter 4, note 10.

13. Hugh J. Murphy, "For Better Yields of Sweet Corn: Feed the Crop," *Maine Farm Research* 4 (1956): 3.

14. Kenneth Ramsey, "Prime Season Nears End at Freedom Cannery," *Belfast (Maine) The Republican Journal* 13 October 1966.

15. L. V. Burton, "Corn Shops Down in Maine, Part Two," *Food Industries* 3 (February, 1936): 62.

16. John Gould, "Corn Shops Are Gone," *Christian Science Monitor* 15 September 1972.

17. Burton, "Corn Shops-Part Two," 62.

18. Richard A. Crabb, *The Hybrid-Corn Makers: Profits of Plenty* (New Brunswick, N.J.: Rutgers University Press, 1947), 262.

19. Earl May, *The Canning Clan* (New York: Macmillan Company, 1937), 52.

20   Russell Bailey. See Chapter 4, note 2.

21. Henry A. Wallace and Earl N. Bressman, *Corn and Corn Growing* (New York: John Wiley and Sons, Inc., 1928), 204.

22. Commissioner of Agriculture, *Agriculture of Maine, Twenty-seventh Report* (Augusta, Maine: State of Maine, 1936), 37; *Agriculture of Maine, Twenty-eighth Report* (Augusta, Maine: State of Maine, 1938), 40.

23. W. E. Schrumpf and Winston E. Pullen, *Costs and Returns in Sweet Corn Production-Central Maine - 1955* Agricultural Experiment Station Bulletin 550 (Orono, Maine: University of Maine, 1956), 14.

24. North Central Regional Fruit and Vegetable Technical Committee, *Marketing Midwest Sweet Corn* North Central Regional Publication 86, Agricultural Experiment Station, Bulletin 530 (Madison, Wis.: University of Wisconsin, 1958), 8.

25. Marshall Edwards. See Chapter 3 note 28. Interview by author 18 February 2000.

26. Schrumph and Pullen, *Costs and Returns*, 10.

27. Ibid.

28. Charles Merchant, *Prices on Farm Products in Maine* Agricultural Experiment Station Bulletin 364 (Orono, Maine: University of Maine, 1933), 12.

29. Richard Condon, "Nearing the End: Maine's Rural Community 1929-1945," *Maine Historical Society Quarterly* 31 (1992).

30. For an excellent overview of the transformation of Vermont see Jan Albers, *Hands on the Land: A History of the Vermont Landscape* (Cambridge, Mass.: The Massachusetts Institute of Technology Press, 2000). Although she makes no mention of the scattered corn canneries in that state, the work offers much to those with an interest in farm operations and small towns of the region.

31. *Pittsfield(N.H.) Valley Times* 17 October 1936.

32. *Pittsfield (N.H.) Valley Times* 17 October 1941.

33. Richard Wescott and David Vail, "The Transformation of Farming in Maine, 1940-1985," *Maine Historical Society Quarterly* 28 (1988).

34. Milton Harris, dairy farmer and sweet corn grower. Interview by author, New Sharon, Maine, 7 February 2000.

35. Charles Bailey, Manager, Monmouth Canning Company, "Report to the Board of Directors of the Monmouth Canning Company, December 19, 1963," files of the Monmouth Canning Company in collection of Peter Soule, Union, Maine.

36. Nancy Bazilshuk, "Essex Man Knows Value of his 91 Years," *Burlington (Vermont) Free Press* 28 February 2000.

37. Peter Mills II is an attorney, member of the Maine Senate and worked in a corn shop. He has a long-standing interest in the history of wages and graciously provided the author with insight on trends in Maine. Telephone interview by author, Cornville, Maine, 20 March 2000. Also see Maine Department of Labor, *History of Maine and Federal Minimum Wage 1938 to September 1997* (Augusta, Maine: Department of Labor, 1997).

38. Almora Warren and James Warren were employed for many seasons at the canning factory in Pittsfield, N.H. Interview by author, Chichester, N.H. 1 April 2000.

39. Jeanette Stevens worked in a corn shop in Farmington, Maine. Telephone interview by author, Temple, Maine, 7 May 2000.

40. Nellie Frederic, see Chapter 4, note 12.

41. Jules J. Arel, "German Prisoners on War in Maine: 1944-1946" *Maine Historical Society Quarterly* 31 (1992).

42. Max Matijczyk, former prisoner of war guard stationed in Maine late in World War Two, interview by author, Newport, Maine, 8 March 2000.

43. Edward Conant worked at the cannery in Randolph, Vt., interview by author, Randolph, Vt., 18 March 2000.

44. Compiled by author based on recall of former corn shop workers.

45. Stevens; Linwood Currier was employed at the cannery in New Sharon, Maine. Interview by author, New Sharon, Maine, 1 March 2000.

46. Sayward Hackett worked at the corn shop in Starks during the 1940's and 50's. Interview by author, Industry, Maine, 1 March 2000.

47. Mary Croswell worked at a corn shop in Farmington, Maine, during World War Two. Letter to author 4 February 2000.

48. R. Gould.

49. Author notes from meeting of the Norridgewock Historical Society, 31 August 1999.

50. R. Gould.

51. Steve Smith, "Corn Shop Days Remembered," *North Conway (N. H.) Reporter*, 20 January 1988.

52. Clyde Davis, superintendent of Burnham & Morrill (later A. L. Stewart) cannery in South Paris, Maine. Interview by author, Norway, Maine, 14 March 2000.

53. Donald Welch worked at cannery and clothespin factories in

Waterbury, Vt. Interview by author, Duxbury, Vt., 18 March 2000.

54. Alberta Currier worked at the cannery in New Sharon, Maine. Interview by author, New Sharon, Maine, 1 March 2000.

55. Author notes from meeting of the Norridgewock Historical Society, 31 August 1999.

56. R. Gould.

57. Murphy, "For Better Yields," 3.

58. R. M. Bailey "Hybrid Sweet Corn: Trends and Problems," paper presented at Farm and Home Week, Orono, Maine 1949.

59. Winston E. Pullen, *Marketing Maine Canned Sweet Corn* Maine Agricultural Experiment Station Bulletin 548 (Orono, Maine: University of Maine, 1956), 15.

60. R. A. Kelly, *The Vegetable Canning Industry in Illinois: Methods of Procurement, Types of Pack, Sales and Distribution, Contacts With Growers* Agricultural Experiment Station Bulletin 612 (Urbana, Ill.: University of Illinois, 1957), 15.

61. North Central Regional Fruit, 5.

62. Helene Kardell, "Hoopeston, Illinois, A Town, A Squalid Camp," *Urbana, (Illinois) Daily Illini,* 29 April 1972.

63. Edward C. Collins and Job K,. Savage, Jr., *Costs of Canning Sweet Corn at Selected Plants*, Marketing Research Report 184, Farmer Cooperative Service (Washington, D.C.: United States Department of Agriculture, 1957), iii.

64. John Gault, "New England Sweet Corn Story," Maine Canners and Freezers Association, 1958.

65. Pullen, *Marketing Maine*, 29.

66. Ibid., 28.

67. John W. Alexander, *Economic Geography* (Englewood Cliffs, N.J.: Prentice-Hall, 1963), 406.

68. Wells. See Chapter 4, note 23.

69. *Maine Register, State Year Book and Legislative Manual* Portland, Maine: Fred Tower Companies, (1920), 57; (1940), 21; (1950), 17; (1960), 15.

70. Commissioner of Agriculture, *Maine Department of Agriculture Biennial Report, 1962-64* (Augusta, Maine: State of Maine, 1964), cover-i.

71. "New England Canners Committee Report," February 11, 1958 provided by Norman Elliott, see Chapter 4, note 24.

CHAPTER 6

People and Corn Shops

1. Allen Wyman, interview by author, Farmington, Maine, 9 February 2000.

2. Milton Harris, see Chapter 5, note 34.

3. Francis Fenton worked one season (1930) at the Mercer shop and thinks the corn shop is the best thing that ever happened in the town. Interview by author, Mercer, Maine, 6 February 2000.

4. Max Matijizyk, see Chapter 5, note 42; A. Wyman; Lois Seamon, interview by author, Chesterville, Maine, 17 February 2000.

5. Phil Andrews, dairy farmer and sweet corn grower. Interview by author, Fryeburg, Maine, 21 March 2000.

6. Ephraim Jillson, see Chapter 4, note 47.

7. Peter Soule, part owner of Monmouth Canning Company, interview by author, Union, Maine, 11 April 2000.

8. Ernest Hilton, ed. *The People and Places of Starks* (State College, Pa.: Jostens, 1995), 118.

9. Edward Jones, interview by author, Fryeburg, Maine, 11 February 2000.

10. Clyde Davis, see Chapter 5, note 52.

11. Marshall Edwards, see Chapter 3, note 28.

12. *Maine Department of Labor, History of Maine and Federal Minimum Wage 1938 to September 1997* (Augusta, Maine: Department of Labor, 1997).

13. Alfred Hurwitz, *History of Liberty*, Maine: 1827-1975 (Liberty, Maine: Liberty Historical Society, 1975), 50.

14. Arthur Hill, see Chapter 4, note 54.

15. Eula Knowlton, interview by author, Freedom, Maine, 15 February 2000.

16. Thelma Bean, interview by author, Starks, Maine, 15 February 2000.

17. Evangline Matijczyk, interview by author, Newport, Maine, 8 March 2000.

18. Stanley Linscott, interview by author, Winthrop, Maine, 29 February 2000. Mr. Linscott passed away soon after the interview.

19. Lawrence Day, interview by author, New Sharon, Maine, 7 February 2000.

20. Pauline Wyman, interview by author, Farmington, Maine, 1 March 2000.

21. Loraine Hodges, interview by author, Windham, Maine, 22 February 2000.

22. Sayward Hackett, see Chapter 5, note 46.

23. Gladys Lovell, interview by author, Madison, Maine, 19 March 2000.

24. Edgar Reed, interview by author, Chichester, N.H., 1 April 2000.

25. Rodney Porter, interview by author, New Sharon, Maine, 4 March 2000.

26. Austin Wood, interview by author, Montpelier, Vt., 18 March 2000.

27. Almora Warren and James Warren, see Chapter 5, note 38.

28. Orland Seamon, interview by author Chesterville, Maine, 17 February 2000.

29. Barbara McGrath, interview by author, Duxbury, Vt., 18 March 2000.

30. Glen Fitch, interview by author, New Sharon, Maine, 10 February 2000.

31. Peter Mills II, see Chapter 5, note 37.

32. Stanley Nightingale, interview by author, New Sharon, Maine, 1 March 2000.

33. Lloyd Perkins, interview by author, New Sharon, Maine, 10 February 2000.

34. Robert Abare, interview by author, Moretown, Vt., 18 March 2000.

35. Clarence Holbrook, interview by author, Auburn, Maine, 21 February 2000.

36. Linwood Currier, interview by author, New Sharon, Maine, 1 March 2000.

37. Donald Welch, see Chapter 5, note 53.

38. Dennis Brown, telephone interview by author, Raleigh, N.C., 10 April 2000.

39. Edward Conant, see Chapter 5, note 43.

40. Ina Porter Turner, interview by author, Farmington, Maine, 17 March 2000.

41. Frank O. Brown, see Chapter 5, note 10.

42. Max Matijczyk, see Chapter 5, note 42.

43. The author thanks Tom Freese, owner of the cannery in Pittsfield, N.H., for providing a tour of the building.

44. Tom Molloy, "Housing Ministry Takes Over Starks Corn Shop," *Waterville (Maine) Morning Sentinel* 19 November 1994.

45. "Helping Hand Thrift Store," *Waterville (Maine) Morning Sentinel* 18 October 2000.

46. John A. Jakle and David Wilson, *Derelict Landscapes: The Wasting of America's Built Environment* (Savage, Md.: Rowman and Littlefield, 1992), 86-91.

47. Steve Bull, "Symbol of Past is Now a Memory," *Farmington (Maine) Franklin Journal*, 13 March 1998.

References

Agriculture Experiments, Progress of. Agricultural Experiment Station
Bulletin 221, Durham, N.H.: University of New Hampshire,
1924.

Alber, Jan. *Hands on the Land: A History of the Vermont Landscape.*
Cambridge, Mass.: Massachusetts Institute of Technology
Press, 2000.

Alexander, H. G. and Paul Reiter. *Report on the Excavation of Jemerz
Cave, New Mexico.* University of New Mexico Bulletin 278,
Albuquerque, N.M.: University of New Mexico Press, 1935.

Alexander, John W. *Economic Geography.* Englewood Cliffs, N.J.:
Prentice-Hall, 1963.

Arel, Jules J. "German Prisoners of War in Maine: 1944-1946." *Maine
Historical Society Quarterly* 34 (1995): 178-193.

"Average Water Balance Data for the Continents, Part Six, North
America (Excluding the United States)." *Publications in
Climatology* 17 (1964): 234-414.

"Average Climatic Water Balance Data of the Continents, Part Seven,
United States." *Publications in Climatology* 17 (1964): 419-
615.

Ayers, Gleason. "Business and Industry." In *History of Waterbury, Vermont, 1915-19*, 222-226. Waterbury, Vermont: Historical
Society, 1991.

Bailey, Charles. "Report to Board of Directors of the Monmouth Canning Company." Monmouth Canning Company files, Collection of Peter Soule, Union, Maine.

Bailey, R. M. "Hybrid Sweet Corn: Trends and Problems." Paper presented at Maine Farm and Home Week, Orono, Maine, 1949.

Bailey, R. M., R .G. Creech, J. J. Natti and R. J. Snyder. *A Regional Approach to Breeding and Testing of Sweet Corn in the Northeast.* Agricultural Experiment Station Bulletin 704, University Park, Pa.: Pennsylvania State University, 1963.

Bangor (Maine) Industrial Journal, 1888-1918.

Baxter, James P. "A Brief History of the Canning Industry in Maine." In *First Bienniel Report of the Commission of Sea and Shore Fisheries of the State of Maine, 1918,* 5-6. Auburn, Maine: Merrill and Webber Company, 1919.

Bazilchuk, Nancy. "Essex Man Knows the Value of His 91 Years." *Burlington (Vt.) Free Press,* 28 February 2000.

Bennett, Randall H. *Bethel, Maine: A Illustrated History.* Bethel, Maine: Bethel Historical Society, 1991.

Bibber, Joyce. "Nearly All in The Family: Nathan Winslow and His Family Network." *Maine Historical Society Quarterly* 28 (1989): 178-193.

Bidwell, Percy and John J. Falconer. *History of Agriculture in Northern United States.* New York: Peter Smith, 1941.

Black, John D. *The Rural Economy of New England.* Cambridge, Mass: Harvard University Press, 1950.

Boswell, Victor R. "Vegetables." In *Yearbook of Agriculure: Soils,* 692-698. Washington, D.C.: United States Department of Agriculture, 1957.

Brady, N. C., R. A. Struchtemeyer and R. B. Musgrave. "The Northeast." In *Yearbook of Agriculture: Soil,* 598-619. Washington, D.C.: United States Department of Agriculture, 1957.

Brown, Elspeth. "Gender and Identity in Rural Maine Women and *The Maine Farmer*, 1870-1875." *Maine Historical Society Quarterly* 33 (1993): 120-133.

Brown, Lawrence. A. *Innovation Diffusion: A New Perspective.* New York: Methuen, 1981.

Brown, Martin, Jens Christiansen and Peter Philips. "The Decline of Child Labor in the U. S. Fruit and Vegetable Canning Industry: Law or Economics." *Business History Review* 66 (1992): 723-770.

Bull, Steve. "Symbol of the Past is Now a Memory." *Farmington (Maine) Franklin Journal*, 13 March 1998.

Bunce, Michael and Gerald Walker. "The Transformation of Rural Life: The Case of Toronto's Countryside." In *Contemporary Rural Systems in Transition: Volume Two, Economy and Society,* edited by Ian Bowler and M. Duane Nellis, 49-61. London: CAB International, 1992.

Bunting, W. H. *A Day's Work: A Sampler of Historic Maine Photographs, 1860-1920, Part Two.* Portland, maine: Maine Preservation, 2000.

Burnham and Morrill Papers. Collection of Richard Gould, Farmington, Maine.

Burton, L. V. "Corn Shops Down in Maine." Parts One and Two. *Food Industries* 3 (January 1936): 9-11; (February 1936): 62-64.

Candolle, Alphonse De. *Origin of Cultivated Plants.* New York: Hafner Publishing Company, 1886.

Canners Directory, 1967-1968. Washington, D.C.: National Canners Association, 1967.

Carlson, Albert and John Weston. "The Sweet Corn Industry of Maine." *Economic Geography* 10 (1934): 382-394.

Carter, Douglas B. "Modern Climatic Classification: Competition or Evolution." *Publications in Climatology* 19 (1966): 309-325.

Carter, George F. "Sweet Corn Among The Indians." *Geographical Review* 38 (1948): 206-221.

Castetter, E. F. and W. H. Bell. "Pima and Papago Indian Agriculture." *Inter-American Studies One,* 85-90. Alburquerque, N.M.: University of New Mexico Press, 1942.

Collins, Edward C. and Job K. Savage Jr. *Costs of Canning Sweet Corn at Selected Plants* Farmer Cooperative Service, Marketing Research Report 184. Washington, D.C.: United States Department of Agriculture, 1957.

Collins, James H. *The Story of Canned Foods.* New York: E. P. Dutton Company, 1924.

Condon, Richard H. "Living in Two Worlds: Rural Maine in 1930." *Maine Historicl Society Quarterly* 25 (1985): 58-87.

——————"Nearing the End: Maine's Rural Community 1929-1945." *Maine Historical Soceity Quarterly* 31 (1992): 142-173.

Croswell, Mary P. Letter to author, 4 February 2000.

Crabb, A. Richard. *The Hybrid Corn Makers: Profits of Plenty.* New Brunswick, N.J.: Rutgers University Press, 1947.

Daniels, Thomas L. and Mark Lapping. "Small Town Triage: A Rural Settlement Policy for the American Midwest." *Journal of Rural Studies* 3 (1987): 273-280.

Darlington, Roy. "Businesses Occupy Former Franklin Farms Site." *Farmington (Maine) Franklin Journal*, 10 March 1995.

Day, Clarence A. *Farming In Maine, 1860-1940*. Orono, Maine: University of Maine Press, 1963.

Durand, Loyal, Jr. "Cheese Region of Southeastern Wisconsin." *Economic Geography* 15 (1939): 283-292.

——————"Cheese Region of Northwestern Illinois." *Economic Geography* 22 (1946): 24-37.

Erwin, A. T. "Sweet Corn - Its Origin and Importance As An Indian Food Plant in the United States." *Iowa State College Journal of Science* 8 (1934): 385-389.

——————"Anent the Origin of Sweet." *Iowa State College Journal of Science* 16 (1942): 481-485.

——————"Sweet Corn Not an Important Indian Food Plant in the Pre-Columbian Period." *Journal of the American Society of Agronomy* 39 (1947): 117-121.

—————— "Sweet Corn - Mutant or Historic Species?" *Economic Botany* 30 (1951): 302-306.

Fernald, Bert M. "Maine Canning Industry." In *Three Able Addresses Delivered Before the State Board of Trade at Bangor, Maine*, March 25, 1902, 3-8. Portland, Maine: Mark Printing, 1902.

Ferwerda, John A., Kenneth J. LaFlamme, Norman R. Kallock Jr. and Robert V. Rocke. *The Soils of Maine*. Agricultural and Forest Experiment Station Miscellaneous Report 402. Orono, Maine: University of Maine, 1997.

Forhan, Henry L. *Revolver for Processing Canned Goods, Patent Number 900,064*. Washington, D.C.: United States Patent Office, 1908.

Frederic, Nellie. Scrapbook. Private Collection of Madge Frederic, Starks, Maine.

Frederic, Paul B. "Historical Geography of The Northern New England Sweet Corn Canning Industry." Master's thesis, Southern Illinois University, 1968a.

Sweet Corn Canning Industry." Master's thesis, Southern Illinois University, 1968a.

————"Historical Geography of The Northern New England Sweet Corn Canning Industry." Paper presented at the meeting of the West Lakes Division of the Association of American Geographers, Madison, Wis., 18 October 1968b.

————"Pre-Canning Antiquity of Sweet Corn." Paper presented at the meeting of the Illlinois Academy of Science, Decatur, Ill., Fall 1969.

————"An Analysis of Spatial Disappearance: The Case of Dairying in a Cash Grain Region." Ph.D. dissertation, University of Illinois, 1973.

————"Rural Industrial Development: The Case of Vegetable Canneries in Maine, 1860-1930." Paper presented at the meeting of the Eastern Historical Geographers, Geneseo, New York, 24 September, 1983.

————"Canners of Gold: Northern New England Corn Shop Workers:1860-1968." Paper presented at the meeting of the Eastern Historical Geographers Association, Bar Harbor, Maine, 22 October 2000.

————"The Northern New England Sweet Corn Industry and Its Demise." Paper presented at the meeting of the New England-St. Lawrence Valley Geographical Society, Providence, R.I., 29 October 2000.

————"Former Vegetable Canneries in Northern New England:

Resource or Blight?" Paper presented at the meeting of the Association of American Geographers, New York, New York 1 March 2001.

Gault, John W. "New England Sweet Corn Story." Maine Canners and Freezers Association, 1958.

——————Address delivered before the Maine Canners and Freezers Association, 11 February 1958.

——————Secretary of the Maine Canners and Freezers Association. Letter to F. Webster Browne, 2 May 1962.

Gerdes, J. T. and W. F. Tracy. "Diversity of Historically Important Sweet Corn Inbreds as Estimated by RELPs, Morphology Isozyms and Pedigree." *Crop Science* 34 (1994): 26-33.

Gould, John. "Corn Shops Are Gone." *Christian Science Monitor*, 19 September 1972.

Gregor, Howard F. *Geography of Agriculture: Themes in Research.* Englewood Cliffs, N.J.: Prentice-Hall, 1970.

Groth, Paul and Todd W. Bressi, eds. *Understanding Ordinary Landscapes*. New Haven, Conn.: Yale University Press, 1997.

Hall, P., ed. *von Thunen's Isolated State.* Translated by Carla M. Watenbery. Oxford: Pergamon, 1966.

Halsted, Byron D., ed. *Barns, Sheds and Outbuildings: Placement, Design and Construction.* 1881. Reprint, Brattleboro, Vt.: Stephen Green Press, 1980.

Hart, John Fraser. "Land Use Change in a Piedmont County." *Annals of the Association of American Geographers* 70 (1980): 492-525.

——————*The Rural Landscape.* Baltimore, Md.: John Hopkins Press, 1998.

Hedricks, U. P. *A History of Horticulture in America to 1860.* New York: Oxford University Press, 1950.

"Helping Hand Thrift Store." *Waterville (Maine) Morning Sentinel,* 18 October 2000.

Hemp, Michael K. *Official Cannery Row Visitors Guide: A Shopping, Dining and Activities Guide to John Steinbeck's Historic Cannery Row.* Monterey, Calif.: Cannery Row Company, 1998.

Hendry, G. W. "Archeological Evidence Concerning the Origin of Sweet Maize." *Journal of the Society of American Agronomy* 22 (1930): 508-514.

Herwig, Wesley. *Early Photographs of Randolph, Vermont: 1859-1948.* Randolph Center, Vt.: Greenhills Books, 1986.

Hilton, Ernest, ed., *The People and Places of Starks.* State College, Pa.: Jostens, 1995.

Hounsell, Janet. M. and Ruth B. D. Horne. *Conway, New Hampshire: 1765-1997.* Portsmouth, N.H.: Peter Randall Publisher, 1998.

Hubka, Thomas C. *Big House, Little House, Back House, Barn: The Connecting Farm Buildings of New England.* Hanover, N.H.: University Press of New England, 1984.

Hudson, John. *Plains Country Towns.* Minneapolis, Minn.: University of Minnesota Press, 1985.

Huelsen, Walter A. *Sweet Corn.* New York: Interscience Publishers, 1954.

Hurwitz, Alfred. *History of Liberty, Maine: 1827-1975.* Liberty, Maine: Liberty Historical Society, 1975.

Ilbery, Brian and Ian Bowler. "From Agricultural Productivism to Post-productivism." In *The Geography of Rural Change,* edited by Brian Ilbrey, 57-85. London: Longman, 1998.

Jakle, John A. and David Wilson. *Derelict Landscapes: The Wasting of America's Built Landscape.* Savage, Md.: Rowman and Littlefield Publishers, 1992.

Jennings, John. *Apparatus for Steaming and Processing Canned Goods, Patent Numner 740,981.* Washington, D.C.: United States Patent Office, 1903.

Jewett Collection. Maine Historical Society Library, Portland, Maine.

Johannessen, Sissel and Christine A. Hastorf. "Corn Culture in Central Andean Prehistory." *Science* 244 (1989): 690-692.

Judge, E .S. "American Canning Interests." In *One Hundred Years of American Commerce,* edited by Chancy M. DePew, 396-400. New York: D. O. Hayes and Company, 1895.

Kardell, Helene. "Hoopeston, Ill. A Town, A Squalid Camp." *Urbana (Ill.) Daily Illini,* 29 April 1972.

Kelley, Isabel and Edger Anderson. "Sweet Corn in Jalisco." *Annals of the Missouri Botanical Garden* 30 (1943): 405-412.

Kelly, R. A. *The Vegetable Canning Industry in Illinois: Methods of Procurement, Types of Pack, Sales and Distribution Contracts With Growers.* Agricultural Experiment Station Bulletin 612. Urbana, Ill.: University of Illinois, 1957.

Langley, Miles E. Representative of the Portland Packing Company. Letter to W. E. Elwell, 22 Novermber 1924.

Lanigan, James W. Minutes of the Maine Canners Association, 17 December 1919.

——— Minutes of the Maine Canners Association, 28 June 1921.

——— Minutes of the Maine Canners Association, 29 March 1922.

Lewthwaite, Gordon R. "Wisconsin Cheese and Farm Type: A

Locational Hypothesis." *Economic Geography* 40 (1947): 95-112.

Lombard, Lucina H. "How a Big Industry Started Near Portland." *Portland (Maine) Sunday Telegram,* 20 October 1907, 11-15.

Magoon, C. A. and C. W. Culpepper. "The Relation of Seasonal Factors to Quality of Sweet Corn." *Journal of Agricultural Research* 33 (1926): 1042-1072.

Maine, Bureau of Industrial and Labor Statistics, *Report of the Bureau of Industrial and Labor Statistics for the State of Maine, 1900 (Fourteenth Annual).* Augusta, Maine: Kennebec Journal, 1901.

Maine, Commissioner of Agriculture. *Agriculture of Maine.* Augusta, Maine: State of Maine, 1919.

——————*Agriculture of Maine, 1922-1925.* Augusta, Maine: State of Maine, 1924.

——————*Twenty-seventh Report.* Augusta, Maine: State of Maine, 1936.

——————*Twenty-eighth Report.* Augusta, Maine: State of Maine, 1938.

Maine, Department of A*griculture, Biennial Report, 1962-64.* Augusta, Maine: State of Maine, 1964.

Maine, Department of Labor, *History of Maine and Federal Minimum Wage, 1938 to September 1997.* Augusta, Maine: Maine Department of Labor, 1997.

Maine Farmer. 14 November 1868; 12 January 1882; 16 March 1882; 22 June 1882.

Maine Register, State Year Book and Legislative Manual. Portland Maine: Fred Tower Companies, 1873; 1880; 1890; 1900; 1910; 1920; 1930; 1940; 1950; 1960.

May, Earl C. *The Canning Clan.* New York: Macmillan Company, 1937.

Mangelsdorf, Paul C. *Corn: Its Origin, Evolution and Improvement.* Cambridge, Mass.: Belknap Press of Harvard University, 1974.

————— "The Origin of Corn." *Scientific America* 255 (1986): 80-86.

Mangelsdolf, Tom. *A History of Steinbeck's Cannery Row.* Santa Cruz, Calif.: Western Tanager Prss, 1986.

McIntire-Swain Camp records. Waterford, Maine, 1912.

Merchant, Charles. *Prices on Farm Products in Maine.* Agricultural Experiment Sation Bulletin 364. Orono, Maine: University of Maine, 1933.

Molloy, Tom. "Housing Ministry Takes Over Starks Corn Shop." *Waterville (Maine) Morning Sentinel,* 19 November 1994.

Morgan, W. B. and R. J. C. Munton. *Agricultural Geography.* New York: St. Martin's Press, 1971.

Morrill, Charles S. *B. and M: What Two Young Maine Men Founded 80 Years Ago.* New York: Newcomer Society of North America, 1950.

Morris, C. and N. J. Evens. "Research on the Geography of Agricultural Change: Redundant or Revitalized?" *Area* 31 (1999): 349-358.

Morse, T. L. S. "Black and Gay Marks Half a Century of Canning." *Rockland (Maine) Courier Gazette,* 16 Novmber 1961.

Mosier, J. G., title unknown. Agricultural Experiment Station Bulletin 208. Urbana, Ill.: University of Illlinois, 1918.

Murphy, Hugh J. "For Better Yields of Sweet Corn: Feed the Crop." *Maine Farm Research* 4 (1956): 3-5.

New England Canners Committee Report, 11 February 1958.

New Hampshire Register, State Year Book and Legislative Manual. Portland, Maine: Fred Tower Companies, 1910; 1920; 1930; 1940; 1950; 1960.

Noble, Allen G. and Richard K. Cleek. *The Old Barn Book: A Guide to North American Barns and Other Farm Structures.* New Brunswick, N.J.: Rutgers University Press, 1995.

Norcliff, Glen. "Canada in a Global Economy." *Canadian Geographer* 45 (2001): 14-30.

North Central Regional Fruit and Vegetable Technical Committee. *Marketing Midwest Sweet Corn.* Agricultural Experiment Station, North Central Regional Publication 86, Madison, Wis.: University of Wisconsin, 1958.

"Obituaries." *Farmington (Maine) Franklin Journal,* 25 February 2000.

"Obituaries." *Waterville (Maine) Morning Sentinel,* 13 February 2000; 25 February 2000; 23 March 2000; 12 April 2000; 4 May 2000; 24 June 2000; 27 June 2000; 18 September 2000; 31 October 2000; 16 December 2000; 16 January 2001; 5 February 2001; 7 February 2001.

Pickard, Samuel T. "Portland." In *Historic Towns of New England* edited by Lyman P. Powell, 53-80. New York: G. P. Putnam's Sons, 1899.

Pittsfield (N.H.) Valley Times, 17 April 1936; 3 October 1941.

Polk, Ralph B. *Apparatus for Treating Canned Goods, Patent Number 742,488.* Washington, D.C.: United States Patent Office, 1903.

Pullen, Winston E. *Marketing Maine Canned Sweet Corn.* Experiment Station Bulletin 548. Orono, Maine: University of Maine, 1956.

Pudup, Mary Beth and Michael J. Watts. "Growing Against the Grain:

Mechanical Rice Farming in the Sacremento Valley, California." In *Comparative Farming Systems,* edited by B. L. Turner and S. B. Brush, 345-384. New York: Guilford Press, 1987.

Radcliffe, Jane E. "Perspectives on Children in Maine's Canning Industry, 1907-1911." *Maine Historical Society Quarterly* 24 (1985): 362-391.

Ramsey, Kenneth. "Prime Season Nears End at Freedom Cannery." *Belfast (Maine) Republican Journal,* 13 October 1966, B-1.

Rolde, Neil. The *Baxters of Maine: Downeast Visionaries.* Gardiner, Maine: Tilbury House Publishers, 1997.

Sanderson, Burton. "Diary For 1890-1900." Collection of David Sanderson, Waterford, Maine.

Sanford, E. F. and C. T. Peggett. *Map of Farmington, Maine.* Philadelphia, Pa.: F. Bourguin, 1874.

Sauer, Carl O. "The Morphology of Landscape." *University of California Publications in Geography* 2 (1925): 19-54.

————"American Agricultural Origins." *Essays in Anthropology Presented to A. L. Kroeber in Celebration of His Sixtienth Birthday June 11, 1936.* 279-297. Berkeley, Calif.: University of California Press, 1936.

————"Theme of Plant and Animal Destruction in Economic History." *Journal of Farm Economics* 20 (1938): 765-775.

———— *Agricultural Origins and Dispersals: The Domestication of Animals and Foodstuffs.* Boston, Mass.: Massachusetts Institute of Technology Press, 1952.

Sax, Karl. *Sweet Corn Breeding Experiments.* Agricultural Experiment Station Bulletin 332. Orono, Maine: University of Maine, 1926.

Schrumpf, W. E. and Winston E. Pullen. *Costs and Returns in Sweet Corn Production - Central Maine.* Agricultural Experiment Station Bulletin 550. Orono, Maine: University of Maine, 1956.

Skowhegan (Maine) Independent Reporter, September 1916.

Smith, Frank W. *Apparatus for Treating or Sterilizing Canned Food, Patent Number 664,642.* Washington, D.C.: United States Patent Office, 1898.

Smith, S. S. "The Growing of Sweet Corn for Canning." In *Twenty-fifth Annual Report of the Maine Board of Agriculture,* 121-136. Augusta, Maine: Sprague and Son, Printers for the State, 1881.

Smith, Steve. "Corn Shop Days Remembered." *North Conway (N.H.) Reporter*, 20 January 1988, 1-3.

Soule, Chester C. "Growth of the Corn Canning Industry." 1909 Paper, Monmouth Canning Company files. Collection of Peter Soule, Union, Maine.

Spencer, Joseph E. and Ronald J. Horvath. "How Does An Agricultural Region Originate?" *Annals of the Association of American Geographers* 53 (1963): 79-92.

Starrs, Paul F. *Let The Cowboys Ride: Cattle Ranching in the American West.* Baltimore, Md.: John Hopkins Press, 1998

Steinbeck, John. *Cannery Row.* New York: Viking Press, 1945.

Storper, Michael. "The Limits to Globalization: Technology Districts and International Trade." *Economic Geography* 68 (1992): 60-93.

Strange, Marty. *Family Farming: A New Economic View.* Lincoln, Neb.: University of Nebraska Press, 1988.

Talbot, Richard F. "The Sweet Corn Industry of Maine." Bachelor's thesis, University of Maine, 1907.

Thompson, George, ed. *Landscape in America*. Austin, Tex.: University of Texas Press, 1995.

Troughton, Michael. "From Nodes to Nodes: The Rise and Fall of Agricultural Activity in the Maritime Provinces." In *Geographical Perspectives on the Maritime Provinces,* edited by Douglas Day, 25-46. Halifax: St. Mary's University Press, 1988.

Turner, Ina Porter. Interview by Naomi Schalit. *Corn Canning in Maine*. Maine Public Broadcasting Corporation, 26 June 2000.

Underwood, W. Lyman. "Incidents in the Canning Industry of New England." In *A History of the Canning Industry and Its Most Prominent Men.* edited by Arthur J. Judge, 12-14. Baltimore, Md.: National Canners and Allied Associations, 1914.

United States, Bureau of Census, *Census of the United States, Manufacturers.* Washington, D.C.: United States Government Printing Office, 1880; 1890; 1900; 1905; 1910; 1914; 1919.

United States Department of Agriculture, *Census of Agriculture, Maine.* Washington, D.C.: United States Government Printing Office, 1899; 1909; 1919; 1924; 1929; 1934; 1939; 1944; 1949; 1954; 1959; 1964.

——————*Census of Agriculture, New Hampshire.* Washington, D.C.: United States Government Printing Office, 1899; 1909; 1919; 1924; 1929; 1934; 1939; 1944; 1949; 1954; 1959; 1964.

——————*Census of Agriculture, Vermont.* Washington, D.C.: United States Government Printing Office, 1899; 1909; 1919; 1924; 1929; 1934; 1939; 1944; 1949; 1954; 1959; 1964.

——————*Commercial Vegetables.* Statistical Bulletin 132. Washington, D.C.: Department of Agriculture, 1953.

——————*Vegetables for Processing.* Statistical Bulletin 411. Washington, D.C.: Department of Agriculture, 1967.

──────── *Vegetable Statistics.* Statistical Bulletin 32. Washington, D.C.: Department of Agriculture, 1928.

Vermont Year Book. Chester, Vt.: National Survey Company, 1930; 1940; 1950; 1960.

Vickery, James Berry III. *A History of the Town of Unity, Maine.* Manchester, Maine: Falmouth Publishing House, 1954.

Wallace, Henry A. and Earl N. Bressman. *Corn and Corn Growing.* New York: John Wiley and Sons, 1928.

Walton's (Vermont) Register, Business Diretory, Almanac and State Year Book. Rutland, Vt.: Tuttle Company, 1910; 1920.

Washburn, Frank P. *Agriculture of Maine: Twenty-ninth Report of the Commissioner of Agriculture of the State of Maine.* Augusta, Maine: State of Maine, 1940.

Wellhausen, E. J., L. M. Roberts and E. Hernandez X. *Races of Maize in Mexico.* Cambridge, Mass.: Bessy Institute of Harvard, 1952.

Wescott, Richard and David Vail. "The Transformation of Farming in Maine, 1940-1985. *Maine Historical Society Quarterly* 28 (1988): 66-84.

Whitman, William E. S. *The Wealth and Industry of Maine, First Annual Report.* Augusta, Maine: State of Maine, 1873.

Will, George F. and George E. Hyde. *Corn Among the Indians of the Upper Missouri.* Lincoln, Neb.: University of Nebraska Press, 1917.

Wilson, Harold Fisher. "The Roads of Windsor." *Geographical Review* 21 (1931): 379-397.

──────── *The Hill Country of Northern New England.* New York: Morningside Heights Columbia University Press, 1936.

Winslow, John M. "Our Canning Interests." In *Agriculture of Maine, Forty-fourth Annual Report.* 198-199. Augusta, Maine: State of Maine, 1901.

Winslow, N. and Company, "Early Corn Canning." 1888 Paper, Maine Historical Society Library, Portland, Maine.

Winslow, N. and Company. Maine Historical Society Library, Portland, Maine

Witthoft, John. *Green Corn Ceremonialism in the Eastern Woodlands.* Ann Arbor, Mich.: University of Michigan Press, 1949.

Zelinsky, Wilber. *Exploring The Beloved Country: Geographic Forays into American Society and Culture.* Iowa City, Iowa: University of Iowa Press, 1994.

Other Materials

The author conducted 75 interviews, many of which are cited in the notes. They provided insight about the sweet corn canning industry. Uncited interviews, miscellaneous printed items, personal correspondence and visits to old corn shops added much to the study's context.

Index

127-128, 140, 142, 145
Wood, Austin, 140
wool, 3
Working Farmer, 36
Works, Will, 146
World War One, 49-50, 52, 69,
    70
World War Two, 83, 100-101,
    103-104, 119, 138-139, 148.
    See also prisoners of war
Wyman, Allan, 117
Wyman, Pauline, 139

X, E. Henandez, 14

yardmaster, 135
Yarmouth, Maine, 28
yield of sweet corn, 37, 73, 75,
    85, 85, 105-106
York County, Maine, 44, 46

Zea mays sccharate. See sweet
    corn
zinc oxide. *See* corn black

About the Author

Paul B. Frederic is currently Professor of Geography at the University of Maine at Farmington. In 1990-91, he was honored with the university's endowed Libra Award. He grew up in Starks, Maine, a corn shope town, where he presently resides. After graduating from the University of Maine at Farmington, he received a M.S. from Southern Illinois University and a Ph.D. from the University of Illinois; all degrees were in geography. Frederic has dairy farmed and served as Director of the Maine Land Use Regulation Commission. His teaching appointments include universities in the Midwest, New York State and Namibia, Africa.

Frederic served as President of the New England-St. Lawrence Valley Geographical Society, and in a variety of positions with the Association of American Geographers - Chair of the Rural Development and History of Geography Specialty groups; Council member; and member of Archives and Association History and the Long Range Planning Committees. Other professional duties have included: Co-coordinator of the Maine Geographic Alliance, and a variety of state and local government committees. Frederic's professional interests focus on rural issues and historical geography. Some of his publications have dealt with arid land grazing systems in Africa, land use planning, forest management policy, historical geography and U.S. - Canadian agriculture.